PRACTICE
MAKES
CATHOLIC

JOE PAPROCKI

PRACTICE MAKES CATHOLIC

MOVING FROM A LEARNED FAITH TO A LIVED FAITH

LOYOLA PRESS.
A JESUIT MINISTRY
Chicago

LOYOLA PRESS.
A JESUIT MINISTRY

3441 N. Ashland Avenue
Chicago, Illinois 60657
(800) 621-1008
www.loyolapress.com

In accordance with c. 827, permission to publish is granted on January 19, 2011 by the Rev. Msgr. John F. Canary, Vicar General of the Archdiocese of Chicago. Permission to publish is an official declaration of ecclesiastical authority that the material is free from doctrinal and moral error. No legal responsibility is assumed by the grant of this permission.

Cover design by Loyola Press
Interior design by Loyola Press

Bible selections are from the New Revised Standard Version of the Bible, copyright 1989 by the Division of Christian Education of the National Council of the Churches of Christ in the USA. Used by permission. All rights reserved.

Cartoons: Copyright © Doug Hall, 1991. Used by Permission.

Library of Congress Cataloging-in-Publication Data
Practice makes Catholic : moving from a learned faith to a lived faith / Joe Paprocki.
    p. cm.
    Based on the author's thesis (Doctor of Ministry--University of St. Mary of the Lake, Mundelein, Ill.).
  ISBN-13: 978-0-8294-3322-7
  ISBN-10: 0-8294-3322-8
1. Christian life--Catholic authors. I. Title.
  BX2350.3.P355 2011
  248.4'82--dc22
                                    2010052815

Printed in the United States of America
19 20 21 22 23 24 25 LSC 11 10 9 8 7 6 5

DEDICATION

To my wife Jo

for practicing life and love with me

since we were in high school

CONTENTS

Acknowledgments

This book is the result of more than five years of research and study, stemming from the thesis project that I undertook as part of my doctor of ministry program at the University of St. Mary of the Lake, Mundelein, Illinois. I would like to thank the following people for their involvement along the way:

- Fr. Ray Webb and the faculty of the doctor of ministry program at the University of St. Mary of the Lake, Mundelein;

- The directors of religious education of the Southwest Cluster of Parishes in the Archdiocese of Chicago who brainstormed Catholic practices with me in 2006 as I began this project;

- The parish RCIA teams in the Archdiocese of Chicago who piloted a spiritual mentoring process using my prototype of *Practice Makes Catholic* in 2006-07: St. Symphorosa, St. Mary Star of the Sea, and Most Holy Redeemer;

- Fr. Mike Nacius, for serving as my DMin project advisor and Dr. Jim Campbell for serving as my theological advisor;

- Frances Cook for editing my thesis paper;

- My doctor of ministry classmates with whom I "traveled" for two years;

- Loyola Press for making the doctor of ministry experience possible for me and for supporting me throughout the program;

- Marge Garbacz (DRE of St. Symphorosa, Chicago) and Cathy Crino (DRE of St. Alphonsus, Chicago) for their very thorough and thoughtful catechetical and pastoral readings of the manuscript for this book and for their excellent suggestions on how to improve it;

- Vinita Hampton Wright, for her excellent editing of the manuscript;

- and, as always, my wife, Jo, for steadfastly standing by me through all of my endeavors!

All It Takes Is a Little Practice

Can you imagine having corrective eyeglasses prescribed for you but choosing to wear them only on the day you purchased them and then once a week for an hour or so on Sundays?

No doubt, seeing clearly each day of the week would be a struggle. And yet, unfortunately, this is what many of us do with our baptism, which is Jesus' vision for life. We "put on" the eyes of Christ on the day of our baptism and then on Sunday when we attend church. Yet, the rest of week, we find ourselves struggling to see as Jesus sees.

Jesus offers us a new way to see—a new way of seeing ourselves, others, life, and God. It is this way of seeing—this vision for life—that the Catholic Church believes and teaches. Like putting on corrective eyeglasses each day, we must also "put on" Christ each and every day so that our vision will be shaped in order to conform to the eyes of God. This Catholic way of seeing can be characterized by five distinct qualities that shape the way we live, move, and have our being. They are

- ✚ **A sense of sacramentality**
- ✚ **A commitment to community**
- ✚ **A respect for the dignity of human life and a commitment to justice**
- ✚ **A reverence for Scripture and Tradition**
- ✚ **A disposition to faith and hope, not despair**

Without these five adjustments to our vision, we simply see the way the world sees, and Jesus taught us to see with a new set of eyes. Thankfully, over the past two thousand years, Catholics have developed a rich treasury of practices that enable us to put on the eyes of Christ each and every day of our lives. These practices, which flow specifically from the five characteristics outlined above, can be integrated into our everyday lives where they enable us, not to withdraw from the world or to blend in with the world, but to robustly engage the world in a life-giving way. This robust engagement with the world avoids what theologian Rev. Robert Barron calls "beige Catholicism"—a bland form of Catholicism that blends in with the rest of our increasingly secular society.

If being a Catholic doesn't make a bit of difference in your everyday living, why bother? In this book, *Practice Makes Catholic: Moving from a Learned Faith to a Lived Faith*, I offer twenty-one tried-and-true practices that both flow from and shape the Catholic way of seeing—a way of seeing that can and will make a difference in your life. As you gradually integrate these practices into your way of life, your life will take on new meaning. You will see differently and, as a result, you will live and act differently.

All it takes is a little practice. After all, have we not been taught since childhood that "practice makes perfect?" Although perfection is not humanly possible, the point is well-taken: in order to excel at anything, we need to practice. The same can be said of living the Catholic vision: we need to practice. In essence, practice makes Catholic, and, to practice Catholicism is to move from a learned faith to a lived faith. May this book help you to start preaching . . . through your actions. May you become a daily practitioner of the Catholic faith, seeing with the eyes of Jesus Christ at all times and becoming a new creation through the transforming power of the Holy Spirit!

Consider Sharing the Journey

Since the beginning of the Church, Christians have realized that the spiritual journey is not meant to be walked alone. In your spiritual journey, it is important for you to walk with someone. Perhaps that person can be a spiritual mentor for you—someone who has a sense of direction and can assist you in learning how to incorporate Catholic practices into your daily life. Or, perhaps this is your opportunity to mentor someone else on the spiritual journey, whether informally or as a sponsor in the RCIA or for someone preparing for Confirmation. Just as a carpenter or an interior decorator guides an apprentice into their craft, a spiritual mentor can guide others into the way of life known as Catholicism. As a mentor, you have the opportunity to reflect on how you are integrating Catholic practices into your own life and to share the experience with another, assisting him or her as they attempt to adapt to the Catholic vision. For information and resources about using this book in a spiritual mentoring relationship around Catholic practices, visit www.loyolapress.com/practice-makes-catholic.

PART ONE

A SENSE OF SACRAMENTALITY

When you get down to it, the most important things in life are intangible: love, acceptance, belonging, forgiveness, commitment, and so on. In order to truly encounter these realities, they need to become embodied. For example, for people to encounter and experience forgiveness, the words, "I forgive you" *must* be spoken; perhaps even an embrace is in order. Either way, forgiveness must be embodied and made tangible.

In a similar way, the practicing Catholic relies on tangible, visible signs to encounter the intangible, invisible God. We recognize that the deepest realities of life—the mysteries of life—transcend words. And so the Catholic vision has a sense of sacramentality—a way of using signs, symbols, rituals, and gestures—tangible realities—to communicate the mystery of faith in our daily lives.

In part one, we'll look at the following Catholic practices related to this sense of sacramentality:

Practice 1: Use Sacramentals
Practice 2: Mark Time the Catholic Way
Practice 3: Fast and Abstain
Practice 4: Speak the Language of Mystery
Practice 5: Pray Sacramentally

To share and learn more in a spiritual mentoring relationship about practicing Catholic sacramentality, visit www.loyolapress.com/practice-makes-catholic.

Practice 1

Use Sacramentals

Sacramentals . . . prepare us to receive grace and dispose us to cooperate with it. "For well-disposed members of the faithful . . . sacramentals sanctify almost every event of their lives with the divine grace which flows from the Paschal mystery of the Passion, Death, and Resurrection of Christ. (*Catechism of the Catholic Church*, 1670)

Catholics Did Not Invent Signs and Symbols

In the classic movie *The Wizard of Oz*, Dorothy's companions each sought something that was intangible. The Scarecrow wanted brains (intelligence). The Tin Man wanted a heart (compassion). The Cowardly Lion wanted courage. When at last they reached the Wizard, he presented each of them with tangible signs of the intangible realities they sought: a diploma to represent the Scarecrow's brains and intelligence; a heart-shaped ticking clock to represent the Tin Man's heart and compassion; and a testimonial—a medal—to symbolize the Lion's courage. By virtue of these

tangible signs and symbols, each of Dorothy's companions was able to experience in a more real way the intangible qualities he sought and, in fact, already possessed to some extent. They simply needed to gain awareness of the qualities that were already present.

Outward signs are important to human beings. This is why spouses exchange gifts on Valentine's Day; why children give gifts

to their parents on Mother's Day and Father's Day; why friends give gifts to one another on birthdays. For Catholics, outward signs provide us with tangible ways of encountering the intangible. We call these outward signs sacramentals. Catholics did not invent outward signs; the use of symbols and signs is innately human. It seems only natural, then, to worship God using signs and symbols.

In his book, *The Long Yearning's End*, (Acta Publications) Patrick Hannon, CSC, states that "to be known by the senses is to be loved. And more than anything else, God wants to love and be loved." Through Catholic sacramentality, God's love can be seen, tasted, touched, heard, and even smelled!

> **The use of symbols and signs is innately human.**

Remember how Dr. Seuss's Grinch (*The Grinch Who Stole Christmas*) tried to steal Christmas from the Who's by stealing all the tangible, external trappings of Christmas? He failed because Christmas resided, not in the trappings, but in the hearts of the Who's. In the same way, if some "Grinch" came along and decided to try to steal all of our Catholic sacramentals—holy water, rosaries, statues, medals, scapulars—in hopes of hearing Catholics weeping and moaning because we could no longer encounter God, he would be frustrated by the sounds of Catholics giving praise to God nonetheless. That's because Catholics understand that God is truly encountered in the human heart but that we, as human beings, rely on outward signs as a means of more deeply encountering such inner realities. The ultimate reality we encounter—the mystery of God—is intangible. And so, Catholics turn toward outward signs as a tangible means of encountering the intangible God.

> **Symbolism is no mere idle fancy or corrupt regeneration: it is inherent in the very texture of human life.**
> Alfred North Whitehead

Examples of Sacramentals

Sacramentals can be divided into two categories:

Sacramental Actions

> Making the Sign of the Cross
> Bowing
> Folding hands
> Genuflecting
> Blessings

Sacramental Objects

> Rosaries
> Statues
> Medals
> Scapulars
> Holy water
> Ashes
> Palms
> Oils
> Icons
> Crucifixes
> Church bells
> Candles
> Incense
> Holy Cards

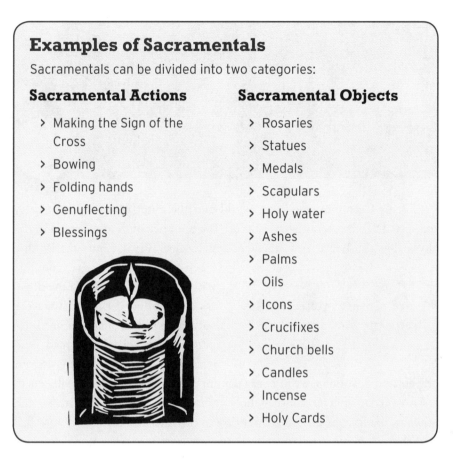

Understanding the Catholic Approach to Sacramentals

In Scripture, encounters with God often involve elements of the natural world: a burning bush, a column of cloud, a pillar of fire, a whispering wind, a mighty wind, and tongues of fire, just to name a few. Perhaps the most familiar example is when God revealed his presence to Moses through a burning bush. This is God's language. God speaks to us using, not only words, but also signs and symbols, objects from the natural world. Like any good parent, then, God teaches us this language. And so, when Catholics use signs and symbols in worship, we are simply speaking the language God taught us. To see the natural world as a reminder and expression of God's presence is to see the world sacramentally.

A woman was praying the Rosary in church when she heard a voice call her name. She tried to ignore it but the voice called out to her several more times. She continued to ignore it and kept praying her Rosary. Finally the voice called her name one more time and said, "I am Jesus!" to which the woman replied, "Shush . . . I'm talking to your mother!"

For us Catholics, the inner world and the outer world are intimately connected. To be sacramental is to see the presence of God reflected in the physical world. Because of this sacramental sensibility, it is no surprise that when we celebrate our encounters with God—the Seven Sacraments—we use ordinary things from the natural world as channels of God's grace: water, oil, fire, bread, and wine. By the same token, in our prayers and devotions, we are very comfortable using images and objects to assist us in our prayer. Statues, holy cards, icons, rosaries, crucifixes, and other sacred images draw our attention to the invisible God. We know full well that when we pray before a statue, we are not praying to or worshipping the statue, and we certainly do not believe that the statue is the manifestation of God or of Mary or the saints. Rather, we use those tangible images to remind us of God's intangible presence in this world. We are simply speaking the language God taught us.

> **We are simply speaking the language God taught us.**

Ash Wednesday—the Most "Catholic" Day of the Year?

We often talk about how some people are "twice-a-year" Christians; they attend church on Christmas and Easter. For Catholics, there is another day that beckons us to return to God by going to Mass: Ash Wednesday. In many ways, Ash Wednesday is the most visibly Catholic day of the year, a day on which Catholic sacramentality literally adorns most Catholics right on their foreheads. Attendance at Mass on Ash Wednesday is typically greater than on certain other holy days of obligation—and Ash Wednesday is not a holy day of obligation! The ashes, made from burning the blessed palms (another sacramental) used on the previous year's Palm Sunday, are placed on our foreheads in the sign of the Cross as a reminder of our mortality and total dependence on God. It is this reminder of our mortality that makes us rethink how we are living at the moment.

Superstition?

When I was a child in Catholic school, I remember being taught that if I got hit by a car and was killed while wearing a scapular (a small sacramental worn around the neck) I would go straight to heaven. It was a very persuasive argument for wearing a scapular, and I recall donning one for a while after that. It sounded like the ultimate insurance policy. But such an approach to sacramentals is superstitious rather than faith-filled. Catholics wear medals and scapulars and dangle rosaries from their rearview mirrors not out of superstition but as reminders of God's ever-present grace. The *Catechism of the Catholic Church* warns us about the dangers of superstition:

> Superstition is the deviation of religious feeling and of the practices this feeling imposes. It can even affect the worship we offer the true God, e.g., when one attributes an importance in some way magical to certain practices otherwise lawful or necessary. To attribute the efficacy of prayers or of sacramental signs to their mere external performance, apart from the interior dispositions that they demand, is to fall into superstition. (2111)

Wearing a scapular is no magical guarantee of getting to heaven; however, it is a practice that reminds us daily to follow Jesus as Mary did, being obedient to God's will, praying always, and tending to the needs of others. These are the activities that lead to heaven.

Another Caution

It's important to understand that when we say we can "find God in all things" we are not equating God with any one thing or object. A beautiful rock or crystal can reflect the beauty and majesty of God, reminding us

"My faith is an important fashion accessory."

of God's presence and majesty. That does not mean that God is in the rock or that the rock is sacred. Some current (and ancient) spiritualities claim that such a rock, stone, or crystal not only reflects God's beauty and majesty but that it is a part of God and therefore possesses healing power or divine energy. This is actually a heresy known as pantheism, which sees God and the world as being one and the same. The movie, *Avatar*, is visually stunning, yet it promotes the notion that nature itself is a divinity to be worshipped. On the other hand, to find God in all things simply means to see the world as a "mirror" that reflects various qualities of God. When we learn to see this way, we develop a deeper respect for all of God's creation and for one another because we realize that these are all opportunities to recognize God in our lives.

The Rosary

Perhaps no other sacramental is associated with Catholics more than the Rosary. For many Catholics, the Rosary is a crucial link to Jesus through the intercession of his mother, Mary. Simply put, the Rosary is a form of meditation. While repeatedly praying the Hail Mary, we are reflecting on specific key moments in the lives of Jesus and Mary. We do so while fingering beads. Remember, the Rosary is a sacramental—a tangible object pointing us to an

But the Rosary Is So Repetitive!

Repetition is a staple of meditation; the repetition of a mantra in Eastern meditation invites us to "lose ourselves" in something bigger than ourselves. If you think that sounds strange, just remember this concept the next time you listen to the great Beatles' song, "Hey Jude." In the latter part of that song, we are invited to repeatedly sing the refrain, "Nah, nah, nah, nah-nah-nah-nah, nah-nah-nah-nah, hey Jude," no less than sixteen times. That's 176 "nahs!" The result is that we become swept up by the music and its repetitive chant. In a similar way, when we pray the Hail Mary, no less than fifty-three times when praying the Rosary, we allow ourselves to get swept away by the story of Jesus Christ.

intangible reality, namely, the Paschal Mystery of Jesus. There is no magic involved. The beads simply guide us in our meditation. Human beings like to keep count. No doubt this is why prayer beads are also found in Islam, Buddhism, Hinduism, and Orthodox Christianity.

How to Pray the Rosary

A Rosary consists of a string of beads and a crucifix. We begin praying the Rosary by holding the crucifix in our hands as we pray the Sign of the Cross and the Apostles' Creed. Following the crucifix, there is

➕ **a single bead (pray the Lord's Prayer),**

➕ **a set of three beads (pray a Hail Mary at each, asking for an increase in faith, hope, and love, followed by the Glory Be to the Father),**

➕ **another single bead (think about the first of the five mysteries you will pray during this Rosary and then pray the Lord's Prayer).**

Next, there is a medal followed by

➕ **five sets of ten beads, each set called a decade,**

➕ **a single bead between each decade on which we think about the next mystery and pray the Lord's Prayer.**

The Mysteries of the Rosary

When I was growing up, there were three sets of Mysteries to reflect on while praying the Rosary: the Joyful, Sorrowful, and Glorious Mysteries (each with five events from the life of Jesus and Mary). Unfortunately, I did not memorize many traditional Catholic prayers and formulas as a child so as an adult, I set out to correct this. During the season of Lent in 2001, I set out to memorize the mysteries of the Rosary. I successfully did so but, the very next year, Pope John Paul II added another set of five mysteries—the Luminous Mysteries. This was the first change in the Rosary in over 400 years. I guess my timing was off by one year! For a full list of the Mysteries of the Rosary, visit www.loyolapress.com/rosary.

We pray a Hail Mary on each bead of a decade as we reflect on a particular mystery in the lives of Jesus and Mary. Pray the Glory Be to the Father at the end of each decade. We end by holding the medal and praying the Hail, Holy Queen and then holding the crucifix as we pray the Sign of the Cross.

God's Fingerprints

It has been said that we human beings are not physical beings in search of a spiritual experience but rather spiritual beings having a physical experience. Catholicism does not seek to escape worldly realities but rather embraces the world that God saw fit to inhabit through his Son, Jesus. Sacramentals are simply worldly objects that remind us of God's presence all around us. When we Catholics look around at this world, we see God's fingerprints everywhere!

Practical suggestions for practicing the use of sacramentals:

> Place a crucifix and a Bible in a prominent location in your home.

> Keep a reminder of your Catholic faith in your workspace and be prepared to explain its significance to those who inquire.

> Carry with you or wear a symbol of your Catholic faith: a medal, a cross, a pin, a scapular, etc. A scapular is made up of two small square or rectangular pieces of cloth, each bearing a religious image, and connected by a string. When placed around one's neck, one square/rectangle rests on the chest and the other on the back. The most popular scapular is the brown scapular of Our Lady of Mount Carmel.

> Look at all of God's creation as sacramental. Remind yourself to look for God's presence in nature and especially in other people.

> Ask yourself at the end of the day where you recognized God's presence.

> Sign yourself with the Sign of the Cross at various moments of your day: as you awake, before and after meals, at bedtime.

> Pray the Rosary, knowing that the fingering of the beads is a concrete way of meditating on the events in the lives of Jesus and Mary.

> When praying the Rosary, focus on the Mysteries that are "assigned" for each day: the Joyful Mysteries (Mondays and Saturdays); the

Luminous Mysteries (Thursdays), the Sorrowful Mysteries (Tuesdays and Fridays); and the Glorious Mysteries (Wednesdays and Sundays).

> Consider placing in your home a small statue or figurine of a favorite saint whose intercession you seek.

> Bring palms home on Palm Sunday and place them in various locations in your home, behind a crucifix or an icon, or on the rear dashboard of your car, and keep them there year-round.

> Keep a small bottle of holy water in your home to bless people and objects.

Scripture

Moses was keeping the flock of his father-in-law Jethro, the priest of Midian; he led his flock beyond the wilderness, and came to Horeb, the mountain of God. There the angel of the Lord appeared to him in a flame of fire out of a bush; he looked, and the bush was blazing, yet it was not consumed. Then Moses said, "I must turn aside and look at this great sight, and see why the bush is not burned up." When the Lord saw that he has turned aside to see, God called to him out of the bush, "Moses, Moses!" And he said, "Here I am." (Exodus 3:1–4)

Prayer

Good and gracious God, you made your presence known to Moses through a burning bush. Help me recognize your presence all around me through the ordinary and extraordinary objects of your creation. May these sacramentals be visible reminders of your invisible yet loving presence.

To share and learn more in a spiritual mentoring relationship about the Catholic practice of using sacramentals, visit www.loyolapress.com/practice-makes-catholic.

Practice 1: Use Sacramentals

Practice 2

Mark Time the Catholic Way

Holy Mother Church is conscious that she must celebrate the saving work of her divine Spouse by devoutly recalling it on certain days throughout the course of the year. (*Constitution on the Sacred Liturgy*, 102)

Living on Borrowed Time

I'm sure you've heard the phrase that a person "is living on borrowed time." We use this peculiar phrase when referring to someone who seems to have cheated death. I say "peculiar" because the phrase implies that the rest of us are living on *our* time, time that belongs to us. In Catholic thinking, there is no such thing as our own time. We believe that all time belongs to God.

In fact, at the Easter Vigil on Holy Saturday, which is the centerpiece of the church year, the priest prays these words as he blesses the Easter candle:

> "Christ yesterday and today, the beginning and the end, Alpha and Omega; all time belongs to him, and all the ages; to him be glory and power through every age for ever."

All of us are living on borrowed time, *all* the time.

But I Thought Today Was November 13!

I was once doing a presentation for a group of IHM (Immaculate Heart of Mary) sisters, and before they introduced me, one of the sisters stood before the group and announced with great joy that "Today is the feast of St. Frances Xavier Cabrini, the first American citizen to be canonized a saint and the foundress of the Missionary Sisters of the Sacred Heart." I thought to myself, *Gosh, if someone asked me what day it was today I would have said, "November 13!"* The sisters were obviously marking time the Catholic way. The Church's liturgical calendar is a reminder to us that all time belongs to God. And so, we do not identify days simply by the month of the year and the day of the week but in relation to events in the lives of Jesus, his mother Mary, and the saints who follow him.

As Catholics, we believe that all time is sacred.

For Catholics, time takes on a unique sense in the context of liturgy and worship. When we enter liturgy, the time that we mark with clocks and watches, *kronos*, is suspended. At that point, *kairos*, which is eternal time or "heaven's time," overshadows our time and invites us to enter God's "eternal now." This eternal now is experienced by the Church through the Church's liturgical year, which is comprised of two cycles. The *temporal* cycle counts the time and the seasons based on the Sundays of the year. The *sanctoral* cycle celebrates the feasts of the saints and holy ones throughout the year. Let's take a closer look at the seasons of the Church's temporal cycle.

All time belongs to God.

➕ **Advent, which begins four Sundays before Christmas and marks the beginning of the Church year, is a time of hope and joyful anticipation in which we prepare to celebrate the birth of Jesus and rejoice in Christ's coming in history, in our encounters with Christ in the present, and in Christ's coming at the end of time.**

➕ **Christmas, a season that includes the celebrations of Jesus' birth (Christmas) and his becoming known to the world (Epiphany), lasts until the feast of the Baptism of the Lord.**

➕ **Lent, a forty-day season of conversion that begins on Ash Wednesday, is a time of turning toward God in preparation for Easter. We do this by praying, fasting, and giving alms.**

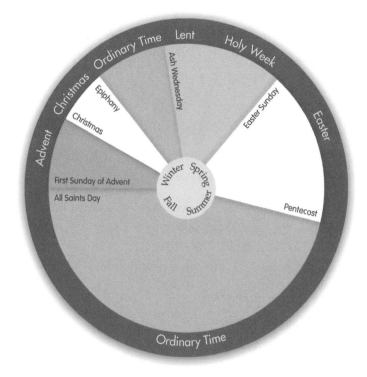

- ➕ Holy Week is our entering into the events surrounding the suffering and death of Jesus, beginning with his triumphant entrance into Jerusalem on Palm Sunday and proceeding through the Triduum, the "three days" of Holy Thursday, Good Friday, and Holy Saturday.

- ➕ Easter is a fifty-day season in which we celebrate Jesus being raised from the dead, which is the central mystery of the Christian faith. Easter is celebrated on the first Sunday after the first full moon of spring.

- ➕ Pentecost is the day on which we celebrate the coming of the Holy Spirit upon the disciples; this occurred fifty days after Jesus' Resurrection. With this feast, the Easter season ends.

- ➕ Ordinary Time is the time set aside for celebrating our call to follow Jesus day by day as his disciples. The Sundays of the entire year are counted (thus, ordinal or ordinary) or set aside as sacred time. Ordinary Time (either thirty-three or thirty-four weeks) is celebrated following the Christmas season and then again following Easter.

Telling Time the Catholic Way

So for Catholics, every single day of the year—the Church's liturgical year—has a connection to Jesus. In this temporal cycle, we identify, first of all, the Sundays of the year. For example:

✚ **the 2nd Sunday of Advent**

✚ **the 5th Sunday of Lent**

✚ **the 3rd Sunday of Easter**

✚ **the 23rd Sunday of Ordinary Time.**

Each of those Sundays has a corresponding set of Scripture readings assigned to them in the lectionary, the sacred book used at Mass from which the Word of God is proclaimed. The lectionary is arranged in a three-year cycle of readings with each year drawing heavily from a particular Gospel:

✚ **Year A: the Gospel of Matthew**

✚ **Year B: the Gospel of Mark**

✚ **Year C: the Gospel of Luke**

A bartender notices that every evening, without fail, one of his patrons orders three beers. After several weeks of noticing this pattern, the bartender asks the man why he always orders three beers. The man says, "I have two brothers who have moved away to different countries. We promised each other that we would always order an extra two beers whenever we drank as a way of keeping up the family bond." Several weeks later, noticing that the man only ordered two beers, the bartender said, "Please accept my condolences on the death of one of your brothers. You know, the two beers and all . . ." The man replied, "You'll be happy to hear that my two brothers are alive and well . . . It's just that I, myself, have decided to give up drinking for Lent."

What Year of the Cycle Are We in Now?

One way to determine what year of the cycle we are in is to divide the 4 digits of the year by the number 3 (note that, although the liturgical year begins in Advent, you'll want to use the year that begins on January 1 immediately following Advent):

> those that are evenly divisible by 3 begin year C;

> those that have a remainder of 1 begin Year A;

> those that have a remainder of 2 begin Year B.

For example, the church year of 2025 actually begins with Advent in 2024. The number 2025 is evenly divided by 3 which means that we will be celebrating cycle C for that church year, which begins with Advent in 2024 and extends through the majority of 2025.

> Weekday Scripture readings follow a two-year cycle referred to as Year I and Year II. Odd number years are Year I and even number years are Year II.

To learn more about the Church's liturgical calendar, go to http://www.loyolapress.com/liturgical-year.htm

The Gospel of John appears occasionally in all three years of the cycle, especially during the Easter season, and appears during Lent of Year A and often during Year B because Mark's Gospel is so short. Many Catholics read, pray, and study Scripture based on this cycle of readings, using the Scripture readings for the upcoming Sunday as the focus of their study.

As for weekdays, they are also identified in relation to the previous Sunday. For example:

➕ **Tuesday of the 3rd week of Advent**

➕ **Saturday of the 2nd week of Lent**

➕ **Monday of the 6th week of Easter**

➕ **Tuesday of the 18th Sunday in Ordinary Time**

In addition to the Church's temporal cycle, the Church's sanctoral cycle designates many days of the Church calendar as days to celebrate Mary and the saints. On these days, it is customary for Catholics to devote their attention to the witness provided by these saints and to draw inspiration and guidance from their lives for following Jesus more closely. And so, for example, Catholics recognize the following dates (just to name a few) as opportunities to celebrate the following saints:

✚ **January 1: Mary, the Mother of God**

✚ **March 19: St. Joseph**

✚ **April 29: St. Catherine of Siena**

✚ **June 29: Sts. Peter and Paul**

✚ **July 31: St. Ignatius of Loyola**

✚ **October 4: St. Francis of Assisi**

✚ **November 30: St. Andrew**

✚ **December 13: St. Lucy**

In many countries, Catholics celebrate special customs related to the lives of saints. For example, on October 4, it is customary to have a blessing of pets in honor of St. Francis of Assisi, who had a great love of animals and showed great care for God's creation.

"As we enter Advent, I'd like to remind the congregation that I can't stand fruitcake."

Liturgy of the Hours

For many years, a friend of mine was a participant in a Catholic-Muslim dialogue. He related how, at various meetings of their group, the Muslims would pause for prayer at specific times while the Catholics stood around and ate cheese and crackers! How ironic, he thought, since the concept of marking time with prayer had deep roots in Christianity and Judaism before Islam made it a pillar of the Muslim faith.

We know from Scripture that it was common for the Jewish people to sanctify their day by praying at certain hours. In the Acts of the Apostles, we find that the first Christians continued this practice. For Catholics and many other Christians, this time-honored way of marking time has come down to us as the Liturgy of the Hours.

The Liturgy of the Hours, also known as the Divine Office, consists of readings in the middle of the night (Matins), a morning prayer of praise (Lauds), an evening prayer (Vespers), and night prayer (Compline). Men and women living in monasteries may even assemble at three other times for prayer. The psalms form the heart of the Liturgy of the Hours, all 150 being prayed over four weeks. This liturgy also includes poetic texts from the Old and New Testaments, other Scripture readings, hymns, intercessions, and the Lord's Prayer. Priests, deacons, and members of religious communities pray the Liturgy of the Hours as part of their spiritual discipline. Lay Catholics are also welcome to incorporate the Liturgy of the Hours into their

The Angelus

One way of marking time throughout the day is the praying of the Angelus at morning (6 a.m.), noon, and evening (6 p.m.). This prayer recalls the words the angel spoke to Mary at the Annunciation:

V   The Angel of the Lord declared unto Mary.
R   And she conceived of the Holy Spirit. Hail Mary . . .

V   Behold the handmaid of the Lord.
R   Be it done unto me according to thy word. Hail Mary . . .

V   And the Word was made Flesh.
R   And dwelt among us. Hail Mary . . .

V   Pray for us, O Holy Mother of God.
R   That we may be made worthy of the promises of Christ.
V   Let us pray. Pour forth, we beseech Thee, O Lord, Thy grace into our hearts; that, we to whom the Incarnation of Christ, Thy Son, was made known by the message of an Angel, may by His Passion and Cross, be brought to the glory of His Resurrection. Through the same Christ our Lord.

All   Amen.

life of prayer and worship. Even when prayed individually, the Liturgy of the Hours becomes a communal act, joining the minds and hearts of countless numbers of people around the world at specific times of the day.

Time and Stewardship

When something does not belong to us, we often take better care of it than we would if it was our own. When we are entrusted with the property of someone else, we become a steward. Because time is something that belongs to God, we are called to be stewards of God's time. In fact, stewardship is the recognition of our responsibility to care for and share what God has entrusted to us: time, talent, and treasure. The Catholic approach to time is a constant reminder that all time belongs to God, and we are stewards of this wonderfully generous gift.

> "Time is too slow for those who wait, too swift for those who fear, too long for those who grieve, too short for those who rejoice, but for those who love, time is eternity."
> HENRY VAN DYKE

Practical suggestions for marking time:

> Recall that every moment of your life is a gift from God.
> Remind yourself that you are living on borrowed time.
> Pray the Angelus at morning, noon, and evening.
> Acquire a liturgical calendar that can help you keep track of the Church year (an economical version is available from www.ltp.org).
> Follow the Church calendar and pray the Liturgy of the Hours; visit www.universalis.com or www.divineoffice.org. Also, visit www.pray-as-you-go.org and www.sacredspace.ie.
> If you're unable to formally pray the Liturgy of the Hours, mark various points in the day with a pause for brief prayer: morning, noon, meal times, evening, night.
> Learn about the saint whose feast is being celebrated on a particular day. Visit http://www.americancatholic.org/Features/SaintofDay/default.aspx.

> Follow the Church's cycle of Scripture readings for each Sunday. Visit the Sunday Connection at www.loyolapress.com/sundayconnection.

> Incorporate the colors of the Church year in your home, workspace, and/or wardrobe

  > Advent = violet/purple

  > Christmas = white

  > Ordinary Time = green

  > Lent = purple

  > Palm Sunday/Good Friday = red

  > Easter = white

  > Pentecost = red

Scripture

And God said, "Let there be lights in the dome of the sky to separate the day from the night; and let them be for signs and for seasons and for days and years, and let them be lights in the dome of the sky to give light upon the earth." And it was so. (GENESIS 1:14–15)

Prayer

God of all creation, you separated the day from night to mark time, and all time belongs to you. Help me appreciate the gift of time and be a good steward of the time you have blessed me with. Help me use my time wisely and unselfishly and learn from the examples of Mary and the saints to follow you more faithfully. Amen.

To share and learn more in a spiritual mentoring relationship about the Catholic practice of marking time, visit www.loyolapress.com/practice-makes-catholic.

Practice 3

Fast and Abstain

> By fasting we sense a deeper hunger and thirst for God. In a paradoxical way, we feast through fasting; we feast on the spiritual values that lead to works of charity and service. Did not the prophet Isaiah proclaim that such works characterize the fasting that God desires? (*Penitential Practices for Today's Catholics*, Committee on Pastoral Practices, National Conference of Catholic Bishops, 2000)

The Way to One's Heart Is through the Stomach

For years, I have worn running shoes sporting various brand names, one of which is ASICS. I had no idea what ASICS stood for until my brother Tom, an avid runner who happens to speak Latin very well, pointed out that the letters are an acronym for the phrase *anima sana in corpore sano*. In English, this translates to "a sound mind in a sound body." It just so happens that this brand name captures the inter-relatedness of the physical and the spiritual, which is at the heart of Catholicism's sacramental spirituality. As a sacramental people, our belief in the Incarnation brings a heightened awareness of the importance of our physical bodies with relation to spirituality.

For this reason, Catholic spirituality involves our bodies. At Mass, this is reflected in the many different postures we assume: sitting, standing, kneeling, genuflecting, bowing, raising our hands, and so on. When it comes to spirituality, we Catholics do not check our bodies at the door. In fact, it has been and continues to be standard practice in monasteries and in many religious communities to require novices to begin their spiritual journey by engaging in physical practices of working and fasting in addition to prayer. This may seem strange at first glance: why would someone who wants to grow closer to God avoid food for a set period of time as the first step on that journey? Spiritual wisdom tells us that any attempt to follow God more closely requires discipline, focus, and willpower. Before attempting to master one's intangible spiritual desires, however, it makes sense to master some tangible physical desires, the most obvious of which is our hunger.

"I'm the head honcho down at Rodeo Burger. Me and the Grill-ettes want you to call off your group's hunger-thon."

Catholic spirituality involves our bodies.

Psychologist Abraham Maslow's hierarchy of needs teaches that physiological needs must be tended to first before one can progress to paying attention to deeper needs such as self-actualization. This same wisdom is at the heart of the Catholic practice of fasting: the key to moving up the ladder of spiritual mastery begins at the physiological level. The way to one's heart is indeed through one's stomach.

The Eye of the Tiger

In the movie *Rocky III*, heavyweight champion boxer Rocky Balboa (Sylvester Stallone) has lost his edge. He's been easily beating a string of no-name boxers in order to maintain his crown. Finally, he gets called out by a fierce newcomer, Clubber Lang ("Mr. T"), who easily defeats the out-of-shape Rocky. Seeking to regain his edge and his crown, Rocky enlists the help of his former adversary Apollo Creed, to act as his coach. Apollo takes Rocky back to the gym where his career began and tells him to look into the eyes of the young boxers who are vigorously training there, in hopes of making it big someday. Apollo tells Rocky, "See that look in their eyes, Rock? You gotta get that look back, Rock. Eye of the tiger, man."

The "eye of the tiger" is an attitude but one that cannot be separated from the physical discipline required of the athlete. This close relationship between the physical and spiritual/emotional/psychological realities of the athlete was not lost on Rocky's friend Apollo. Nor was it lost on St. Paul, who drew upon the imagery of running and boxing to describe his own spiritual journey:

> Do you not know that in a race the runners all compete, but only one receives the prize? Run in such a way that you may win it. Athletes exercise self-control in all things; they do it to receive a perishable garland, but we an imperishable one. So I do not run aimlessly, nor do I box as though beating the air; but I punish my body and enslave it, so that after proclaiming to others I myself should not be disqualified. (1 CORINTHIANS 9:24–27)

Since biblical times, fasting and abstinence have been viewed as appropriate expressions of repentance for sin. The prophet Isaiah teaches us about true fasting when he asks, "Is it not to share your bread with the hungry, and bring the homeless poor into your house; when you see the naked, to cover them, and not to hide yourself from your own kin?" (58:7). Fasting, therefore, is a very physical way to express the fact that our relationships with God and others need to be healed. Before Jesus began his ministry, he fasted in the desert for forty days and forty nights (Matthew 4:1–2). He was tempted to turn a stone into bread—to take care of his own physical needs. Instead, he remained focused on what truly sustained him: the Word of God. We, too, are tempted to think that many things in life sustain us when truly, God alone sustains us. Through fasting, Catholics learn to practice self-denial, to lead a life of moderation that deepens our compassion for people in need, and to develop a deeper hunger and thirst for God.

Every athlete exercises self-control in all things. (St. Paul)

Fasting is also a form of discipline, a way of admitting that we are tempted with obsessions with food, drink, sex, television, and so on. Through fasting, we strive to bring our relationship with our self into line. For Catholics, fasting is not primarily an individual practice but one that has social implications. While fasting, many Catholics donate the food they would have eaten (or the equivalent value thereof) to an organization that feeds the hungry. In this way, fasting restores our relationship with our neighbors all over the world.

> **"When the stomach is full, it is easy to talk of fasting."**
> SAINT JEROME

Fasting's Cousin: Abstinence

Abstinence refers to refraining from eating meat, a food that symbolizes prosperity. To abstain from meat is to align ourselves with the poor who cannot afford to provide meat for themselves and their families. Fasting and abstaining from meat remind us of our reliance on God, who is the source of all abundance and nourishment. As Catholics, we are encouraged to fast voluntarily and occasionally throughout the year. A day of abstinence is a day (such as the Fridays of Lent) on which Catholics fourteen years or older abstain from eating meat (under the current discipline in America, fish, eggs, milk products, and condiments or foods made using animal fat are permitted in the Western Rite of the Church, though not in the Eastern Rites.) Persons with special dietary needs can easily be exempted by their pastor.

Fasting During Lent

The season of Lent—the forty days before Easter—is the primary time of the year for Catholics to practice fasting and abstaining from meat. In fact, fasting is identified as one of the three "disciplines" of Lent, along with prayer and almsgiving. During the Lenten season, the Church reminds us of "Lenten regulations" regarding fasting and abstaining from meat. Under current canon

Actual announcement in a church bulletin for a National PRAYER & FASTING Conference: "The cost for attending the Fasting and Prayer conference includes meals."

law in the Western Church, a day of fast is one on which Catholics who are eighteen to fifty-nine years old are required to keep a limited fast. In the United States, such a fast is characterized by limiting oneself to a single, meatless meal along with two smaller meals, so long as these smaller meals do not add up to a second meal. Snacking is not allowed. Drinking coffee, tea, juices, etc., between meals is permitted on fast days. Those with medical conditions requiring a greater or more regular food intake can easily be exempted from the requirement of fasting by their pastor.

> **For Catholics, fasting is not primarily an individual practice but one that has social implications.**

The minimum that the Catholic Church expects is for us to fast on Ash Wednesday and Good Friday. But the entire forty-day season of Lent is a good time to practice a limited form of fasting. Other forms of self-denial, within reason, can also be spiritually beneficial at any time. Everyone age fourteen and older is required to abstain from meat on Ash Wednesday and the Fridays of Lent.

Tips for Fasting

> Tell the least number of people that you are fasting (but be sure to tell at least one other person).
> Turn off the TV (commercials and sitting make you hungry).
> Combine your fasting with prayer.
> Designate a purpose for your fast.
> Start by reducing intake and then intensify to skipping one meal each week.
> Increase your liquid intake.
> Use your physical hunger as a reminder of your spiritual hunger for God.
> Fast with others (positive peer pressure).
> Experience solidarity with those who are hungry.
> Donate in money the equivalent of the food you would have eaten.

Exceptions to the Rule

Of course, fasting can have serious implications for people with certain medical conditions. Diabetics, for example, must be very careful about allowing their blood sugar to get too low as a result of fasting. In cases where age or medical condition render fasting dangerous to one's health, common sense dictates that such individuals are exempted from the discipline of fasting. These individuals are encouraged to practice some other form of discipline (penance).

The Friday Fast and the Eucharistic Fast

For many years, Catholics abstained from eating meat on Fridays throughout the year. Although this requirement was lifted in the 1960s, Catholics are still encouraged to engage in some form of fasting and/or abstinence on Fridays in preparation for Sunday, which is always a celebration of Jesus' Resurrection. In memory of Christ's suffering and death, the Church prescribes making each Friday (the day that Jesus died) throughout the year a penitential day.

Likewise, back in the day, Catholics used to prepare for receiving the Eucharist at Sunday Mass by fasting from midnight on! Today, canon law states that we are to fast for at least one hour before receiving Holy Communion. This Eucharistic fast has its roots in Scripture; we are told that the apostles connected worship and fasting (Acts of the Apostles 13:2). This practice once again reminds us that we are to worship God with our whole being: mind, body, and soul. Because fasting is associated with penance and conversion, the Eucharistic fast reminds us that before coming to the Lord, we need to turn away from sin. The physical hunger and thirst that we experience is a sacramental experience; it is a tangible feeling that parallels our spiritual hunger and thirst.

In Scripture, fasting not only was an expression of penance but was also an experience that prepared individuals to be open to God's action. For example, Moses fasted for forty days on Mount Sinai before receiving the Ten Commandments. Jesus himself fasted in the desert for forty days before beginning his public ministry. In the same way, our one-hour fast before receiving the Eucharist prepares us to be open to God's action in our lives. The one-hour time is not something to be followed scrupulously to the second but rather is a suggestion for a significant period of time during which we begin to experience hunger and thirst. I don't know about you, but I can't go much longer than an hour before my stomach starts grumbling!

The Fringe Benefits of Fasting

People who fast regularly will attest to the benefits of this practice, not only for their spiritual lives, but also for their physical well-being. While the goal of fasting is not primarily to lose weight or to sculpt a new body, restricting one's diet does contribute to overall health. In addition to the obvious weight-loss benefits, fasting is known to create a heightened alertness while also cleansing the body of toxins. In the end, the best approach to fasting is not to think of it as depriving yourself of something but of striving for something more!

Breakfast

The word *breakfast* literally means to "break the fast" that we experience from the time of our last meal the evening before until the first meal of the morning. The midnight fast that Catholics used to practice explains why early Masses were (and in many cases still are) so popular for folks who were born in the 1950s and earlier. Going to a 6 a.m. Mass meant breakfast during the 7 a.m. hour!

Practical suggestions for Practicing Fasting and Abstaining from Meat

> Ash Wednesday: This day marks the beginning of the Lenten season. Ash Wednesday is a day of fasting (for those ages eighteen to fifty-nine) and abstinence from meat (for those age fourteen and over).

> Good Friday: Christ suffered and died for our salvation on a Friday. On the Friday that we call "Good," the Church gathers to commemorate Jesus' Passion and death. Good Friday is a day of fast and abstinence (see age restrictions above). The Good Friday fast is the paschal fast—a fast of anticipation and longing for the Passover of the Lord, which should continue, when possible, through Holy Saturday.

> Fridays during Lent: In the United States, we maintain the tradition of abstaining from meat (see age restriction above) on each Friday during Lent.

> Fridays throughout the year: In memory of Christ's suffering and death, the Church prescribes making each Friday (the day that Jesus died) throughout the year a penitential day. For years, Catholics observed Fridays by practicing abstinence from eating meat. Although this requirement was lifted in the 1960s, Catholics are still encouraged to engage in some form of fasting and/or abstinence on Fridays in preparation for Sunday, which is always a celebration of Jesus' Resurrection.

> Fast for one hour before receiving the Eucharist as a way of reminding yourself that God alone can satisfy your every need.

> Fast not only from food but from any behaviors or habits that distract you from following Jesus, such as being judgmental, using inappropriate language, or gossiping.

Scripture

"And whenever you fast, do not look dismal, like the hypocrites, for they disfigure their faces so as to show others that they are fasting. Truly I tell you, they have received their reward. But when you fast, put oil on your head and wash your face, so that your fasting may be seen not by others but by your Father who is in secret; and your Father who sees in secret will reward you." (MATTHEW 6:16–18)

Prayer

Lord, Jesus, you fasted for forty days in the desert, opening yourself up to your Father's will before you began your public ministry. Help me practice fasting with a spirit of openness to the Father's will, so that I may be more sensitive to the needs of others and remain focused on my baptismal call to holiness. Amen.

To share and learn more in a spiritual mentoring relationship about the Catholic practice of fasting and abstaining from meat, visit www.loyolapress.com/practice-makes-catholic.

Practice 4

Speak the Language of Mystery

The need to involve the senses in interior prayer corresponds to a requirement of our human nature. We are body and spirit, and we experience the need to translate our feelings externally.
We must pray with our whole being to give all power possible to our supplication. (*Catechism of the Catholic Church*, 2702-2703)

Do You Know Sign Language?

I often ask Catholics if they know sign language, and most respond by saying, "No." I then proceed to silently make the Sign of the Cross, to genuflect, to bow, to trace the cross, using my thumb, on my forehead, lips, and chest, and to place my hands in the *orans* position (hands slightly extended with palms up). Folks quickly recognize what I am pointing out to them: Catholics *do* know sign language. We are a sacramental people, expressing ourselves beyond words, and relying on signs, symbols, and ritual gestures. Why do we bother? Because words alone are not enough, especially in relationships. Likewise, when it comes to expressing ourselves to God, words alone cannot do justice. We engage our entire bodies in expressing ourselves to God, who speaks to us in ways that transcend words.

This is not a particularly deep theological concept. It's simply very human. When children go to bed at night, they hope to go to sleep knowing that they are loved by their parents. Hearing the words "I love you" is welcome, but a hug is even more appreciated. In fact, a hug is so effective, that it can often be delivered without the accompaniment of words. Of course, when you get the words and the hug together, that's the best of both worlds.

> **When it comes to expressing ourselves to God, words alone cannot do justice.**

God's Language

Catholicism gives us the best of both worlds by providing both words and gestures; they form a language of mystery. Why? Because this is how God revealed himself to us. God is known to us, not only through words, but also and primarily through actions. This is God's language and, like any good parent, he teaches his children how to speak.

This is one of the most profound differences that Catholics encounter when they visit some non-Catholic churches for worship: an entire aspect of God's language is missing. The words prayed and preached may very well be uplifting and inspiring; however, the lack of sacramental language can leave a person feeling like that child I just described, who is sent to bed without a hug. Our spoken language alone is inadequate to express the overwhelming reality of God's mysterious presence.

> **"Grace must find expression in life, otherwise it is not grace."**
> Karl Barth

As Catholics, we pray bodily. We kneel, stand, bow, genuflect, raise our hands, and sign ourselves. Of course it is possible to pray within one's heart without using gestures or bodily movements. However, it is important to remember that our spiritual self is not separated from our physical self. Body, soul, and spirit act as one. In Hebrew, the word for worship (*shachach*) actually means to "bow before" in a posture of submission. To bow to someone or something is to physically orient or align our body with that person or thing. It is to say, in essence, "I direct all of my being—physical, emotional, and spiritual—to you." When we pray with our bodies, we present our entire being to God.

My Dad's Last "Words"

Some years ago, as my dad, suffering from Alzheimer's disease, lay dying in the hospital, I witnessed an extraordinary example of the language of mystery. After slowly deteriorating mentally and physically over the course of a few years,

"Arthur judges a church by the amount of wear on the kneeling pads."

my dad was now unable to communicate with us. His eyes were closed most of the time, and he uttered nothing more than a few indistinguishable grunts every so often. As family and friends came to bid their farewells, we attempted to communicate with Dad, letting him know who was present and what they were saying. No response. Then, my wife and I decided it was time to take our two children, Mike and Amy (then ages twelve and nine), to say goodbye to Grandpa. Still, no response.

But then, during our visit, a priest friend of the family stopped by. After we chatted, he asked if he could say a prayer and we said yes. He raised his hand to make the Sign of the Cross. At that very moment, Dad also raised his hand, and in a very jerky yet unmistakable motion, made the Sign of the Cross. No sooner had we witnessed this than Amy, our youngest child, burst into tears. Somehow, the mystery of the moment had touched both the oldest and the youngest persons in the room, and they responded in the only ways they could: beyond words.

They responded in the only ways they could: beyond words.

While Dad had been seemingly incapable of understanding or communicating anything, he somehow knew that God was present in that hospital room. He responded to that mysterious moment with the only language left to him. His "last words" were not spoken words at all but a gesture that he had learned some seventy-five years earlier. At the same time, our daughter Amy, overwhelmed by the mystery of the moment, responded in the only appropriate manner for a nine-year old: by crying. The rest of us in the room realized that we had encountered a mystery. God's presence had become very real to us, without any words at all. This was not a moment to be solved or explained, only entered into and treasured, which is what we do in the face of mystery.

Elements of the Language of Mystery

God's language of mystery includes a variety of elements. Here are just a few.

Ritual: A good birthday celebration follows a ritual. We celebrate a birthday this year in pretty much the same way we celebrated last year, and the year before that, and the year before that. The ritual includes presenting a birthday cake with candles, singing a simple song, blowing out the candles, opening the presents, and eating the cake. This ritual conveys a deep meaning. It brings comfort. It can evoke very deep emotions. Rituals, both in church and in the home, are an important part of Catholic practice, reminding us of God's presence in every moment of our lives. And so we practice rituals such as lighting Advent candles, marking doorways with chalk on Epiphany, blessing Easter baskets, lighting vigil candles, observing meatless Fridays, and much more.

C + M + B?

One ritual that many Catholics observe each year on the Feast of Epiphany is marking the formula 20 (for the years beginning 20) +C+M+B+ (last two digits of the current year) with chalk above the door. For example, 20+ C+M+B+25 for the year 2025. The C, M, and B represent the traditional names of the Magi: Caspar, Melchior, and Balthasar. These initials also stand for the Latin prayer *Christus mansionem benedicat* or "Christ bless this house." The ritual represents the wish on the part of those who dwell there that all who enter their house during this year will find the newborn king within. It is also a reminder to welcome all visitors with hospitality.

Song: Imagine a birthday party in which people decided to recite "Happy Birthday" instead of sing it. Ugh. It's the singing of the words: "Happy birthday to you, happy birthday to you, happy birthday dear [name], happy birthday to you," that can bring people to happy and sentimental tears. For the same reason, we enjoy musicals, performances in which singing conveys something that the spoken word simply could not. Imagine *The Sound of Music* beginning with Julie Andrews reciting the words, "The hills are alive with the sound of music," instead of singing them. It's just not the same. Singing lifts our minds and hearts in a way that speaking cannot. For Catholics, singing is part of the language of mystery, so much so that the rubrics of the Mass tell us that if, for whatever reason, we are not able to sing the Alleluia at Mass, it should be omitted! Singing is one of the most important things we do as a community during Mass. We sing during the opening procession, we sing the Gloria, the psalm response, and the Gospel acclamation. We sing as the gifts are brought to the altar. We sing the Sanctus (Holy, Holy), the mystery of faith, the Amen, and sometimes even the Lord's Prayer. Finally, after singing the Lamb of God, we sing as we process to Communion and once again as we process forth at the end of Mass. That's a lot of singing, and it's not just frosting on the cake we call liturgy; singing is an essential part of how we worship as Catholics.

> **"Those who sing pray twice."**
> St. Augustine

Silence: There are some moments in life when we need to just shut up. In fact, God says as much, albeit much more diplomatically, when he tells us, "Be still, and know that I am God" (Psalm 46:10). Why? Because silence is part of God's language. We're not talking about creating quiet so as to be able to hear God speaking actual words; we're talking about silence itself being an expression of God's language. At Mass, we sit in silence after each of the Scripture readings and, for a more extended moment, after receiving Christ in the Eucharist. These moments of silence are often my favorite parts of the Mass. In this noisy world of ours, it's not often that we gather with large groups of people and sit in silence. In our private lives, as well, we practice forms of prayer in which silence is a key element. One popular form of silent prayer is centering prayer, a form of prayer in which a person rests in God by focusing on a simple word or image, or by focusing on the breath coming in and going out. By the way, that dialogue bubble off to the side of this page is empty for a reason: it's filled with silence!

Gesture: One of the first questions that non-Catholics have when they begin the RCIA (Rite of Christian Initiation for Adults) process is "what's that thing that you do with your hand right before the Gospel?" Of course, that "thing" is the gesture of tracing the Cross with our thumb on our forehead, lips, and heart, while silently praying the words, "May the Word of God be in my mind, on my lips, and in my heart." This is just one of many gestures and postures that Catholics include in prayer and worship. Here are a few more:

➕ **The Sign of the Cross:** Probably the most recognizable Catholic gesture is the Sign of the Cross. In his book, *The Sign of the Cross* (Loyola Press), Bert Ghezzi tells us that "Fourth-century Father of the Church St. Basil said that the apostles 'taught us to mark with the sign of the cross those who put their hope in the Lord,' that is, those who presented themselves for Baptism" (p. 20). For most Catholics, the Sign of the Cross is the first Catholic gesture learned, at a very early age. Each time we sign ourselves with the Cross, we are asking for God's blessing. We are also welcome to trace the Sign of the Cross on the foreheads of others, something that many parents do for their children, as a way of asking God to bless them.

➕ **Bowing:** to bow is show respect and humility. We bow to the altar in church as we approach our seat or cross in front of the altar. We bow during the Creed at the words, "and by the Holy Spirit was incarnate of the Virgin Mary." We also bow just before receiving the Body and Blood of Christ in Communion.

➕ **Kneeling and Genuflecting:** The knees are symbols of strength. To kneel is to bend our strength before God, on whose strength we rely. Kneeling is also a penitential position. We humbly kneel before God, who showers us with mercy. We genuflect (touch the right knee to the ground) before a tabernacle containing the Blessed Sacrament. We kneel at Mass during the Eucharistic prayer and again from the

How to Make the Sign of the Cross

The Sign of the Cross is made (prayed) by opening up the right hand and, with the tips of the fingers:

> touching the forehead ("In the name of the Father")

> touching the breastbone ("And of the Son")

> touching the left shoulder and then the right shoulder ("And of the Holy Spirit")

> folding the hands together ("Amen").

In Hispanic cultures, it is customary to cross the thumb over the index finger to make a cross and to end the Sign of the Cross described above by kissing the thumb (kissing the Cross) as a sign of veneration for the Cross of Jesus Christ. Eastern Catholics and the Orthodox make the Sign of the Cross by holding the thumb, index finger, and middle together (symbolizing the Trinity) and then tucking the ring finger and pinky toward the palm (representing the two natures of Christ—divine and human). Likewise, Eastern Catholics and Orthodox touch the right shoulder first and then the left shoulder.

Lamb of God through Holy Communion. We can kneel at our own bedside in prayer at the end of the day.

➕ **The *Orans* Position:** The early Christians prayed standing with their hands raised slightly, palms upward, as a sign of openness to God's will. The word *orans* is Latin for "praying." Often during the Mass, the priest prays in the orans position. During the Lord's Prayer, many Catholics assume the orans position. We can pray this way at any time either in public or private.

Talk Is Cheap

Ghandi once said that "it is better to have a heart without words than words without a heart." Catholicism is a way of life that has its own language, a language of mystery that goes beyond words and speaks to and from the heart. God teaches us this language, not only speaking the Word to us, but allowing the Word to become flesh, an expression of God's love for us that took place amidst the silence of that night when Jesus was born.

Lena, who was a successful performer in show business, went to confession one Saturday. She mentioned to Father Sullivan that she was an acrobatic dancer, and he wanted to know what that meant. She said she would be happy to show him the kind of thing she did on stage. She stepped out of the confessional and within sight of Father Sullivan, went into a series of cartwheels, leaping splits, handsprings, and backflips. Kneeling near the confessional, waiting their turn, were two middle-aged ladies. They witnessed Lena's acrobatics with wide eyes, and one said to the other: "It used to be that saying a few Hail Marys on our knees was good enough. Now look at what Father Sullivan is requiring for penance!"

Practical suggestions for practicing the language of mystery:

> Before reading Scripture or any other inspirational literature, trace a cross with your thumb over your forehead, lips, and heart, praying silently, "May the Word of God be in my mind, on my lips, and in my heart."

> Make the Sign of the Cross before meals, even when in public places, as you silently pray grace.

> When praying in private, occasionally lie prostrate before the Lord (lay flat on the floor, face down, with arms outstretched) as an expression of surrender, praise, and humility

> Pray occasionally in the orans position: standing, hands raised slightly with palms upward, as a sign of openness to God's will.

> Kneel at your bedside; this is a traditional prayer posture that expresses humility and contrition.

> Pray as you engage in exercise: bike riding, swimming, walking, running, and so on. Combine the physical exercise with spiritual exercise.

> Many churches and retreat houses have a labyrinth, a single path of concentric circles that leads to a center point and back. This pattern allows you to contemplate while slowly walking the spiritual path that represents the path of life.

> Pay attention to all the ways we pray bodily at Mass: standing, sitting, kneeling, bowing, signing ourselves, and so on.

> Bless yourself with holy water when entering and leaving a church building as a way of reminding yourself of the gift of your baptism. Keep a bowl of holy water in your home and do the same upon entering and leaving your home, which is the domestic church.

> When entering a church and approaching your seat, bow to the altar or, if the Tabernacle is in the sanctuary, genuflect (touch your right knee to the ground) as an expression of reverence for Christ's presence in the Blessed Sacrament.

Scripture

Therefore God also highly exalted him and gave him the name that is above every name, so that at the name of Jesus every knee should bend, in heaven and on earth and under the earth, and every tongue should confess that Jesus Christ is Lord, to the glory of God the Father. (Philippians 2:9–11)

Prayer

Lord, Jesus, I bow before you, praising your Name in word, song, and deed. Help me to learn your language of mystery. Help me to listen to you in the silence and to speak to you with not only my mouth, but with my heart, hands, and my entire self. Help me to enter more deeply into the mystery of your love. Amen.

To share and learn more in a spiritual mentoring relationship about the Catholic practice of speaking a language of mystery, visit www.loyolapress.com/ practice-makes-catholic.

Practice 5

Pray Sacramentally

When we pray to the Father, we are in communion with him and with his Son, Jesus Christ. Then we know and recognize him with an ever new sense of wonder. (*Catechism of the Catholic Church*, 2781)

The Play Is under Review

Football fans have become quite accustomed to the fact that crucial plays will often be reviewed. Under close scrutiny, the replay official may recognize some subtle nuance that determines whether the call on the field stands or is reversed. The fact is, the referees, and most folks in general, often don't see everything the first time around. By reviewing the play, they hope to see more clearly what really happened.

Our life of prayer can work much the same way. By reviewing what has transpired, we can come to see some things that we missed—most notably, God's presence! Unfortunately, many of us grow up with a notion of prayer that is always future oriented. We find ourselves like children sitting on Santa's lap, asking and hoping for good things to come our way in the future. But we actually recognize God more easily in the rearview mirror. We can more easily recognize God's presence in our past than in the present moment.

A Catholic Way to Pray

One form of prayer that is very common for Catholics is reflective prayer, or, prayer that looks back in order to recognize the presence of God in our everyday experiences because we may have missed him the first time around. St. Ignatius of Loyola was a champion of this form of prayer. He called it the *Daily Examen.* In this simple form of prayer, Ignatius encourages us to set aside fifteen minutes (he actually warned his followers not to pray too long!) to review our day, as if pressing the rewind button on a video recording and then watching it in fast-forward. He suggests the following steps:

> **"It's always easier to see God in retrospect."**
> Rev. James Martin, SJ

1. Quiet yourself and recall God's presence, thanking God for his love and asking the Holy Spirit for guidance.

2. Review your day, thanking God for the various blessings you experienced.

3. Review your day again, thinking about the opportunities you had to use the gifts God has given you, identifying the times you either did or didn't.

4. Thank God for the ways you grew closer to him and ask forgiveness for the opportunities you missed or rejected.

5. Resolve to cooperate with God's grace in the day(s) to come and conclude with the Lord's Prayer.

By praying in this manner, we become more aware of how God has been present to us in the past and therefore, more attuned to how he is acting in the present. The result is a new way of seeing, and that's precisely what our sacramental sensibility is—a way of seeing God in all things.

Praying with Imagination

It is said that at her trial for heresy, St. Joan of Arc was told by the inquisitor that, "You say God speaks to you, but it's only your imagination" to which Joan replied, "How else would God speak to me, if not through my imagination?" The fact is, imagination plays a very important part in our prayer life and, because of our sacramental sensibility, we Catholics find ourselves in a unique position to benefit. Once again, we can look to St. Ignatius of Loyola for promoting a form of prayer that encourages us to use all our senses—sight, smell, touch, taste, sound—to imagine ourselves in a setting where we can encounter Jesus. The setting may be from a Gospel story in which we insert ourselves as a character, watching and listening as Jesus acts and speaks and then speaking with him ourselves and listening to what he has to say to us. Likewise, the setting may be a favorite location or a memory that we revisit and invite Jesus into.

Even though our lives can be hectic at times, we don't need to go to a monastery or search for a deserted place in the woods in order to pray imaginatively. We simply need to make a transition of focus so that we can become more in tune with God's presence in our activities. Imaginative prayer involves the following simple steps.

1. Find a quiet place (although with practice, this can even be accomplished on a noisy bus or train) where you can experience solitude for ten or fifteen minutes. Assume a comfortable position and, if you wish, close your eyes or focus on a religious picture or a lighted candle. If you wish, play soft background music to help establish a prayerful mood. Become aware of God's presence and ask the Holy Spirit to guide your prayer.

2. Take two or three minutes to practice rhythmic breathing—counting to three slowly and silently while breathing in and counting slowly to five

5:27 P.M. – S.W. Sneedlap remembers he was created just a little lower than the angels.

while breathing out—to help concentration. If you become distracted, return to concentrating on your breathing and let the distractions go by so that you can turn your heart back to God. Likewise, you can choose a special word or phrase, such as *Jesus* or *My Lord and My God*, and repeat it when you are distracted to bring your attention back to God's presence.

3. Select a brief passage from Scripture and prayerfully read it. If the passage you select is a Gospel story, use your five senses to imagine yourself as a participant in the story (What can you see? What sounds do you hear? What can you feel?).

    > "Grant me, O Lord, to see everything now with new eyes."
    > PEDRO ARRUPE, SJ

    Imagine a setting in which you can talk with Jesus and listen to him speak to you. You can respond to what Jesus is saying or doing in the story, or you can simply talk about something that has happened to you recently or about a forthcoming event in your life.

4. In addition to using Scripture in your reflection, you can also use writings from or about the saints as well as other inspirational literature or prayer books. Likewise, you can choose to concentrate on a sacred object such as a crucifix or reflect on a sacred image, such as an icon of Jesus or a favorite saint. Take this time to talk to God as you would to a friend.

5. Close with one or two minutes of contemplation, time to rest silently in God's presence. As adults, we come to recognize more and more that

Two Jesuit novices both wanted a cigarette while they prayed. They decided to ask their superior for permission. The first asked but was told no. A little while later he spotted his friend smoking and praying. "Why did the superior allow you to smoke and not me?" he asked. His friend replied, "Because you asked if you could smoke while you prayed, and I asked if I could pray while I smoked!"

God speaks to us using the language of silence. Take a few moments at the end of your reflection to spend some silent time with God.

Through imaginative prayer you can begin to more readily recognize God's presence in your daily life.

Devoted to You

In the 1950s, the Everly Brothers had a hit song entitled *Devoted to You*. When was the last time you heard someone use that phrase in describing a relationship?! To devote oneself to someone or something is to concentrate fully and set oneself apart for that someone or something. Ultimately, this is the aim of prayer: to help us concentrate fully and set ourselves apart for God. For this reason, we often refer to our prayers as devotions. While the Church has official prayers such as the Mass and the Liturgy of the Hours, there are also numerous other forms of prayers called devotions that Catholics practice. These devotions often focus on Mary and the saints and how they can help lead us to Christ and follow him more faithfully. Some devotions are prayers such as the Rosary and the Stations of the Cross. Other devotions are focused on the veneration of images such as the Sacred Heart of Jesus or Our Lady of Guadalupe. Others are rituals such as the practice of observing First Fridays, and still other devotions take the form of wearing a sacred object such as a scapular or medal.

One very popular and traditional Catholic devotion, already mentioned, is the Stations (or Way) of the Cross, which combines many different aspects of Catholic

What's a Novena?

One popular Catholic devotion is the novena. The word *novena* means "nine" and is used to describe nine days (or hours) of private or public devotion or prayer for a specific cause. The nine days comes from the time that Mary and the apostles waited in prayer between the Ascension of Jesus and the coming of the Holy Spirit on Pentecost. Novenas can be prayed for mourning a loss or for anticipating an upcoming event or feast. There is no magic involved in novenas. Rather, they are an expression (a sacramental sign) of the intensity of one's prayer. The goal of a novena is to deepen one's devotion to God.

sacramental prayer. Most Catholic churches and chapels have images—either pictures or sculptures—of the fourteen stations of the Cross. These are artists' depictions of fourteen events in the story of Jesus' suffering and death on the Cross. It is customary for Catholics to pray the Stations of the Cross (using a devotional prayer guide) while actually walking from station to station. In this way, our prayer is embodied, as we walk from scene to scene, reflecting on the suffering and death of Jesus. This time-honored devotion thus includes words, images, and movement, involving all of our senses in a meditative walk with Jesus. In essence, the Stations of the Cross prayer is a pilgrimage-in-place, joining us to the Church in the Holy Land, where Christians physically retrace Jesus' way of the Cross.

If These Walls Could Talk . . .

We use the phrase, "if these walls could talk," to describe a place where something significant has occurred—something that would make a great story. Catholic walls CAN and DO talk! Since very early times in the Catholic Church, our sacramental sensibility has led us to use visual images to tell the story of salvation. For centuries, statues, icons, and stained glass windows have catechized (taught) Catholics and inspired prayer. I still vividly recall the huge stained-glass windows in St. Casimir church on the south side of Chicago where I grew up and how these images often

The Church Needs Art

In 2000, Pope John Paul II hosted six hundred artists at the Vatican as part of the celebration of the Jubilee Year. In a letter he wrote to artists, the Holy Father said the following:

"In order to communicate the message entrusted to her by Christ, the Church needs art. Art must make perceptible, and as far as possible attractive, the world of the spirit, of the invisible, of God. It must therefore translate into meaningful terms that which is in itself ineffable. Art has a unique capacity to take one or other facet of the message and translate it into colours, shapes and sounds which nourish the intuition of those who look or listen. It does so without emptying the message itself of its transcendent value and its aura of mystery." (12)

mesmerized me when I was too young to understand what the priest was talking about in his homily.

In our own homes as well, we do not hesitate to incorporate sacred images that transform our homes into a "domestic church"; such images remind us of God's presence and grace. In the home where I grew up, my mother prominently included statues of the Sacred Heart of Jesus and the Immaculate Heart of Mary as part of the living room and dining room décor. These images were not garish or overpowering but understated, a simple expression of our devotion to God.

No, We Don't Worship Icons

St. Basil the Great explained how icons assist us in prayer without leading us into idolatry:

"If I point to a statue of Caesar and ask you 'Who is that?' your answer would properly be, 'It is Caesar.' When you say such you do not mean that the stone itself is Caesar, but rather, the name and honor you ascribe to the statue passes over to the original, the archetype, Caesar himself."

We would say the same thing about an icon: our prayer "passes over" the icon to that which the icon represents.

Windows to Heaven

Sacred icons, an especially important part of Eastern Christian spirituality, are also an important part of Catholic prayer. Icons, often referred to as "windows to heaven," are sacramental; they are visible images that lead us to encounter the invisible God. The concept of icons is inspired by the experience of the Incarnation: that moment when the invisible God became visible in Jesus. Icons are much more than aesthetic pieces of art. Icons can be an important part of our prayer, helping us focus and use our senses to glimpse the divine. We do not worship images but rather venerate them. Worship is directed solely to God. Veneration, or the showing of honor and respect, can be directed to persons or objects who lead us to God. When Catholics pray using statues, icons, or other images, we use those objects to help us focus on what they point to.

When praying with an icon, rather than closing our eyes, we pray with our eyes wide open. The goal of such prayer is to meditate on the image, taking in what the image is expressing to us and on what we see in it and through it. Praying with an icon is a form of prayer without words, leading us to simply rest in God's presence. When praying with an icon, we may light a candle and gaze upon the icon in silence, allowing it to connect us to Jesus and the communion of saints. As we gaze and slowly breathe in and out, we listen with our hearts, not our ears, to what God is saying to us.

I'll Light a Candle for You

Catholics are very big on lighting candles. One of the distinguishing characteristics of traditional Catholic churches is the presence of rows of flickering votive candles (some churches now use electric candles because of fire codes and insurance regulations). These candles are intimately related to our practice of prayer and the notion of interces-

> **When praying with an icon, rather than closing our eyes, we pray with our eyes wide open.**

sion—praying on behalf of someone else. Most often, these votive candles are found in front of a statue or icon of the Blessed Virgin Mary or one of the saints with whom we join our prayer, asking them to intercede for us or for the person for whom we are praying. The lit candle is a symbol (a sacramental) of the persistence of our prayer, expressing our desire that our prayer continue even after we leave and go about our daily business. When we walk into a church and see rows of flickering votive candles, we are immersed in the prayer of the community. It is common for Catholics, when offering comfort and support to someone in need, to say, "I'll light a candle for you" as a way of assuring someone of not only our prayers, but of the intercession of Mary and the saints.

How Much Does Prayer Cost?

Some people develop the mistaken notion that Catholics are paying for their prayers when they light a votive candle in church and then place money in the offering box of the candle stand. The money is not an attempt to bribe God! It is simply an offering to offset the cost of the candles provided by the church.

This practice of lighting candles as part of our prayer carries over into the homes of Catholics, where we often light votive candles to give thanks to God or to ask for the intercession of Mary and the saints for a particular cause that is dear to us. This practice is especially popular in various ethnic groups as a sign of devotion to local patron saints and in relation to various apparitions of Mary.

So, the next time you are with someone who is in need of prayers, tell them, "I'll light a candle for you."

Practical suggestions for practicing sacramental prayer:

> Practice the Daily Examen, a prayerful review of your day, each evening during your commute home from work or before you retire for the night.

> Pray imaginatively with the upcoming Sunday Gospel reading, using all your senses to enter into the story and to interact with Jesus.

> Learn about devotions that are unique to your own ethnic background. Talk to parents, grandparents, aunts, and uncles to learn about devotions they practice that are part of your ethnic heritage.

> Make it a practice to pray a novena in anticipation of major events in your life. On your calendar, mark off nine days before the event and dedicate yourself to praying in a special manner during those nine days.

> Visit Catholic churches in your community or city and let the walls "talk." Observe the stained-glass windows, statues, icons, sculptures, and other forms of sacred art that speak to us about the Catholic faith.

> Place an icon in your home. Select an icon of your patron saint or a favorite depiction of Jesus or Mary.

> Practice praying with an icon using the steps outlined in this chapter.

> Observe First Fridays, a practice related to the devotion of the Sacred Heart of Jesus, that involves receiving Communion on the first Friday of each month for nine consecutive months (as St. Margaret Mary Alacoque was directed to do in a vision) to reflect on the Lord's Passion. Recall what we said earlier about Friday being the day we recall the Lord's death as well as the number nine (novena) representing our perseverance in prayer.

> The next time you are with someone who is in need of comfort and prayers, tell him or her that you will light a candle for them.

> Each time you enter the church, light a candle either to give thanks to God or to ask for prayers for yourself or someone else.

Scripture

So I will bless you as long as I live;

I will lift up my hands and call on your name.

My soul is satisfied as with a rich feast,

and my mouth praises you with joyful lips

when I think of you on my bed,

and meditate on you in the watches of the night;

for you have been my help,

and in the shadow of your wings I sing for joy. (PSALM 63:4–7)

Prayer

Good and gracious God, thank you for reaching out to me, inviting me to grow closer to you. May my prayer be a heartfelt and sincere response to you. Help me pray with my whole mind, heart, soul, and strength, using all my senses to encounter you. Help me recognize you as I look back on my daily experiences and, in doing so, learn how to see you more clearly in the present moment. Amen.

To share and learn more in a spiritual mentoring relationship about the Catholic practice of praying sacramentally, visit www.loyolapress.com/practice-makes-catholic.

PART TWO

A COMMITMENT TO COMMUNITY

Catholics believe that human beings are created in the image and likeness of God. That means that we share a "family resemblance" with God, not so much on the physical level as on the spiritual level. And it just so happens that the God whom we resemble is Trinitarian, meaning that God's inherent nature is communal: Father, Son, and Holy Spirit—one God, three Persons. God is a community of persons—a community sharing such an intimate relationship, that God is not three but one. Thus, since we are created in the image and likeness of God, we are also inherently communal. We most reflect the divine image when we engage in community. Catholicism, therefore, is not a "me and God" experience, but an experience of finding God in all people. Our commitment to community is so strong that not even death separates us from one another. As a community, we recognize that God is our Father and that we are all brothers and sisters with the responsibility to care for one another.

In this unit, we'll look at the following Catholic practices related to our commitment to community:

Practice 6: Be a Good Steward

Practice 7: Share the Gifts of the Holy Spirit

Practice 8: Pray with the Whole Church

Practice 9: Welcome One Another

To share and learn more in a spiritual mentoring relationship about practicing the Catholic commitment to community, visit www.loyolapress.com/practice-makes-catholic.

Practice 6

Be a Good Steward

Stewardship is not simply making donations or taking care of the building and grounds. It is a spirituality—hence a way of life—made of four parts: receiving the gifts of God with gratitude; cultivating them responsibly; sharing them lovingly in justice with others; standing before the Lord in a spirit of accountability. (*Stewardship and Young Adults*, USCCB)

"Mine!"

We are born completely self-centered. As infants, we cry in order to have all our needs met. As we learn to speak, one of the first words we grasp after "mama" and "papa" is "mine!" If you've ever watched toddlers playing with one another, you know what I mean. All it takes is for one to grab hold of a playmate's favorite toy and the fun begins: "Mine! Mine! Mine!" It is at this point that parents make their best effort to increase their toddler's vocabulary by one more very important word: "share!"

Sharing does not come easily for most of us. Our selfish tendencies are exacerbated by a society that promotes the notion of a "scarcity mentality." On a regular basis, we receive the message: there's not enough to go around, so grab for what you can. Scripture, however, paints a very different picture, one of abundance. Beginning with Genesis, we are taught that God's creation is filled with everything we need, all provided by a generous and loving God who calls us to share with others. Jesus' first miracle, the changing of water into wine at the wedding feast at Cana, reinforces this notion of abundance: the six huge water jars, each capable of holding more than fifty gallons, are filled to the rim. The message? For those who live under God's reign, there is more than enough to go around.

Recognizing the abundance of God's creation is the first step toward sharing with others. However, we also need to realize that when it comes to material possessions, the word "mine" is a misnomer. There really is no such thing as "mine" because everything in God's creation truly belongs to God— who has chosen, in his generous love, to share with us. And so, rather than seeing ourselves as owners, we come to recognize that we are stewards.

> **For those who live under God's reign, there is more than enough to go around.**

Stewardship

In the Nicene Creed, we proclaim our belief in God as the Creator of "all things visible and invisible." In this creed, we are expressing our belief that everything we have is a gift from God. Our response is to live as caretakers of God's gifts and to use them wisely for the good of all. Another word for caretaker is *steward*. Catholics believe that we are called to live as stewards of God's creation, and as stewards we recognize that all we are and all we have belong to God. Since we ultimately have no ownership of anything but are entrusted with the care of that which belongs to God, we try to avoid hoarding anything for ourselves. Stewardship calls us to care responsibly for God's gifts and to share generously of our time, talent, and treasure.

Stewardship, then, is not a parish program, nor is it ultimately about money. It is an attitude and a way of life. Stewardship is a lifestyle that enhances our relationships with God and our brothers and sisters by calling us to center our lives on Jesus rather than ourselves.

"The stewardship committee wants to create an atmosphere of optimism."

Where Do Catholics Stand on Tithing?

Tithing is the act of designating 10 percent of one's income for charity, particularly for one's church. This practice, which is more common in Protestant circles, takes its origins from Old Testament law, which required tithing to maintain the Temple. In essence, this was part of a tax that supported the "governing institution" of Israel. Although Catholics are not bound to the 10 percent rule, we are bound by the Precepts of the Church to "contribute to the support of the Church." If we are financially unable to share a set percentage of our income with the Church, we are still bound to share our time and talents with the community of faith.

➕ **We do so by sharing our time with others, realizing that we are all living on borrowed time.**

➕ **We do so by sharing our talents in service of others, knowing that our talents are gifts from God.**

➕ **We do so by sharing our material possessions, acknowledging that the resources of the earth were created by God for the good of all people.**

Stewardship is not a matter of giving up a portion of what is ours. It's a matter of recognizing that we are blessed to be able to keep a large percentage of what is God's after we've returned to him a small percentage of what already belongs to him!

My Parents: Setting a Good Example

My parents were not rich. As a result, their contributions to the Church were never all that dramatic. We were not poor, but cash flow was limited in a family of nine children. My parents gave what cash contributions they could while spending gobs of money on Catholic school tuition for all nine children. However, their stewardship did not end there. They devoted more than their fair share of time and talent to the parish community. Both Mom and Dad enthusiastically served numerous roles in the parish to practice their stewardship. They must have done a good job of instilling a sense of stewardship in all of us children; we have served or continue to serve as cantors, guitarists, lectors, auxiliary ministers of Holy Communion, catechists, and a variety of ad hoc ministries and services in our various parish communities. Oh yeah, don't forget, one of the nine is a bishop!

By the way, as of the writing of this book, Mom is eighty-four years young and still serving her present parish as a sacristan, lector, auxiliary minister of Holy Communion, and occasional altar server! Stewardship lives on!

Turning in Your Envelope

As a child in a Catholic grammar school, I thought it was so cool when I received my first packet of envelopes. All the grownups had envelopes, and every Sunday at Mass they got to drop their envelopes in the baskets that the ushers passed through the congregation. Now I, too, could drop an envelope with my name on it into the basket. My excitement quickly diminished, however, when I learned that I had to put some of my own money in the envelope!

I'm not sure what I thought was in those envelopes that people were placing in the offering basket, but I sure as heck did not like the thought of dipping into my allowance to contribute. However, my parents taught me that this was part of our responsibility. In fact, for Catholics, the envelope is a very important symbol—not a sacramental per se, but certainly a powerful reminder of our commitment to the community.

Catholics obtain these offering envelopes through an expression of commitment to community, namely, the act of registering as a parishioner. It is very difficult to remain anonymous at a Catholic parish. We are asked to visit the rectory and register as a parishioner, not just so that the parish can get some envelopes into our hands, but as our own expression of commitment to the mission of the Church and to this local community of faith.

Today, envelopes are often replaced by online giving; however, the act of registering as a parishioner remains. One parish I know of makes it clear that parish registration cannot be completed online; it requires a face-to-face at the parish office. The message? We are not anonymous. We are members of a community.

Solidarity: "I'm with You!"

In an episode of *Seinfeld*, Jerry's friend Elaine was looking for clues to reveal whether a good-looking guy she met at the health club liked her or not. She thought she was about to get a clear signal when the guy asked her for a drink from her water bottle. She concluded that sharing a water bottle would be an expression of intimacy. Of course, she was crestfallen when the guy took her water bottle and wiped off the bottle top with his towel before taking a sip!

> **"For it is in giving that we receive."**
> St. Francis of Assisi

For Catholics, one of the most profound expressions of our commitment to community—our relationship with one another—is drinking from the one cup at Mass. By sharing that cup, we express our solidarity with one another. We don't normally drink from a glass, bottle, or can that someone else has been drinking out of. If at all, we may do so with family.

Why Can't We Use Individual Cups Like the Other Parish Does?"

When, as a parish director of religious education, I was preparing children and their parents for First Communion, I demonstrated how the children would receive the Precious Blood from the cup. One of the mothers was very uncomfortable with this. She said, "Why can't we use individual cups like some of the other parishes do?" I had to explain to her that if a church was using individual communion cups, it was *not* a Catholic parish! Drinking from the one cup is a very Catholic notion. It reminds us that Jesus responded to his disciples, who were seeking the best seats in heaven, by asking "Are you able to drink the cup that I am about to drink?" (Matthew 20:22) He was asking them if they were truly willing to bear the burden of commitment. To drink from the cup at Mass is our way of not only receiving our Lord, but also of expressing our commitment to community.

And yet, when we receive Holy Communion—the Body and Blood of Jesus Christ—we drink from the same cup! The message is clear: we are family. We are bound to one another. We are in solidarity with one another, united in the mission of proclaiming the Gospel of Jesus Christ.

Our solidarity, however, is not limited to those who drink from the cup at Mass. We practice solidarity with all of God's people. Our commitment to community is truly catholic—that is, universal. We are called to stand in solidarity with people of every nation, race, creed, and color. And so our stewardship is not limited to parish communities. Rather, our commitment to solidarity calls us to practice stewardship for the good of all people—even people we will never meet.

> **As Catholics, we practice solidarity with all of God's people.**

The notion of solidarity is so important to Catholics that the bishops of the United States included it as one of the seven principles of Catholic social teaching (see practice 12). The bishops describe solidarity in this way:

> We are our brothers' and sisters' keepers, wherever they live. We are one human family, whatever our national, racial, ethnic, economic, and ideological differences. Learning to practice the virtue of solidarity means learning that "loving our neighbor" has global dimensions in an interdependent world. (CATHOLIC SOCIAL TEACHING: SHARING CHALLENGES AND DIRECTIONS, USCCB)

Bottom line? Catholics are not easily deterred by the phrase "mind your own business."

Religious Communities and Poverty, Chastity, and Obedience

Finally, any discussion of the Catholic commitment to community would be incomplete without some mention of the long tradition of religious communities in the Catholic Church. For centuries, men and women have sought to live in communities of faith, following a "rule" and bound together by promises of poverty, chastity, and obedience. What these sisters, nuns, brothers, and monks teach all of us is that these three evangelical counsels are the "glue" of any community and that all of us are called to practice them as they pertain to our state of life.

- ✚ **Poverty:** we are all called to practice a spirit of poverty, detaching ourselves from material possessions so that all of God's people might share in the abundant resources of God's creation. Catholics realize that our true treasure lies in our life with God.

- ✚ **Chastity:** All people are sexual beings, called to relate to others in the appropriate manner, according to our state of life. Faithfulness in our relationships is key to a healthy community.

- ✚ **Obedience:** Obedience does not mean that one person says, "Jump" and the other replies, "How high?" It means that people in a community are accountable to one another. In any community, we voluntarily sacrifice some degree of our individualism for the common good.

And so, we can all look to the many Catholic religious communities—Jesuits, Dominicans, Franciscans, Ursulines, Felicians, Benedictines, Redemptorists, Servites, Carmelites, and Poor Clares, just to name a few—for good examples of what all of us Catholics are called to practice: a commitment to community.

Practical suggestions for practicing stewardship and solidarity:

> Begin each day by giving thanks to God for the many blessings he is sharing with you.

> Remind yourself that all time belongs to God and that you are living on borrowed time. Consider how you can be generous with the time that God has given you today.

> Cultivate a spirit of poverty—a sense of detachment from material goods—realizing that true happiness comes only from God and not from possessions.

> Consider what you are doing or might be able to do to better preserve natural resources and to protect the environment. Do your best to recycle and to avoid being wasteful.

> Keep loose change or small bills with you to assist those in need that you encounter in your daily commute. Or, if you prefer not to give cash, buy booklets of fast-food coupons and offer those to people who seem like they could use a meal.

> When making purchases, ask yourself if this is something that you truly need or if you might be able to use the money for more constructive purposes.

> Reflect on your gifts and talents and ask yourself how you are using them to serve others at home, work, school, and in your community.

> Designate a form of service or community involvement that will allow you to share your time and talent with others

> If you are not registered at a Catholic parish, consider doing so as a sign of your commitment to community.

> If you do not presently drink from the cup at Mass, consider doing so. This is a powerful expression of our commitment to the mission of the Church.

> Designate a percentage of your income to give to charity, including your parish, and try to keep your giving at this level consistently. If cash flow is a problem, consider sharing your time and talents with the community.

Scripture

Now the whole group of those who believed were of one heart and soul, and no one claimed private ownership of any possessions, but everything they owned was held in common. With great power the apostles gave their testimony to the resurrection of the Lord Jesus, and great grace was upon them all. There was not a needy person among them, for as many as owned lands or houses sold them and brought the proceeds of what was sold. They laid it at the apostles' feet, and it was distributed to each as any had need. (ACTS OF THE APOSTLES 4:32–35)

Prayer

Father, Son, and Holy Spirit, you are a community of love, so intimate that you are One. Because I am made in your image, help me live in community with others, sharing loving relationships that reflect your glory. Give me the patience I need to live in community with others and please, Lord, grant patience to those who need to put up with me! Help me share generously of my time, talent, and treasure, and help me live in solidarity with all your children. Amen.

To share and learn more in a spiritual mentoring relationship about practicing stewardship and solidarity, visit www.loyolapress.com/practice-makes-catholic.

.

Practice 7

Share the Gifts of the Holy Spirit

All powerful God, Father of our Lord Jesus Christ, by water and the Holy Spirit you freed your sons and daughters from sin and gave them new life. Send your Holy Spirit upon them to be their helper and guide. Give them the spirit of wisdom and understanding, the spirit of right judgment and courage, the spirit of knowledge and reverence. Fill them with the spirit of wonder and awe in your presence. (Rite of Confirmation)

An Extraordinary Gift

When we receive an extraordinary gift, we generally can't wait to show it to someone. More often than not, we are eager to share this gift with others so that they, too, can enjoy it. When Dad receives a new barbeque grill, he can't wait to have family and friends over for a cookout. When Mom receives a bouquet of flowers, she places it in a vase and sets the vase where family and visitors can enjoy its beauty. When a child receives a new video game, he or she can't wait to invite friends over to join in the fun. Gifts are intended to be shared.

Gifts are intended to be shared.

In Baptism, we receive an extraordinary gift: the Holy Spirit. The presence of the Holy Spirit produces further gifts: wisdom, understanding, reverence (piety), knowledge, fortitude, counsel, and fear of the Lord. When we realize the talents and gifts that the Holy Spirit inspires in us, we respond in humility and gratitude, knowing that we have done nothing to earn these gifts.

To show our gratitude, we use these gifts as they were intended to be used—for the good of others. By sharing our gifts with others, we lose nothing and gain everything. In fact, by trying to horde gifts for ourselves, we lose them.

> "Gratitude does not turn us inward with a sense of passive contentment but points us outward in service. The experience of being gifted fosters a desire to gift others."
>
> GERALD M. FAGAN, SJ,
> *PUTTING ON THE HEART OF CHRIST*

On the Receiving End

Throughout, my life, I have been on the receiving end of others' gifts. In turn, I have learned to share these same gifts with others.

✚ **Wisdom** enables us to see life from God's point of view and to recognize the real value of persons, events, and things.

Fr. Jack Daley taught me how to see William the way God sees him. William was a student of mine and he didn't seem to like me or my class. In turn, I began to dislike him, seeing him as someone who had little value. And then Fr. Jack walked into my room one day at the end of class. He was coming to chat with me but his eye caught William and he turned toward him with a big smile and a warm greeting; William came to life in a way I had never witnessed. Fr. Jack engaged him in discussion and gradually

---

Who is the Holy Spirit?

So, just who is the Holy Spirit—this "gift-giver"? Today, it's common for people to rely on lawyers. Lawyers provide legal guidance and expertise in situations that are too legally complex for us to face on our own. We sometimes refer to lawyers with the title "counselor." The Holy Spirit is our counselor, provided by Jesus to assist us in becoming disciples. Because living as a disciple of Jesus can be challenging, Jesus' Spirit remains with us and provides his gifts to help us when we are sent into the world to live out our calling.

> A catechist asked her students to share some wisdom that they had learned from their parents or grandparents. A young man raised his hand and said, "My grandfather was very wise and he once said, 'People never really listen, they just wait for their turn to speak.' Or at least that's what I think he said. I wasn't really listening."

brought me into it. I saw a part of William I hadn't seen before. From that point on, I began to look at William through Fr. Jack's eyes. Because of Fr. Jack's wisdom—his ability to see from God's point of view—my relationship with William improved, as did his attitude toward me and my class. Because of Fr. Jack's wisdom, I learned how to look for the best in people.

➕ **Understanding** gives us insight into the truths of faith and being a disciple of Jesus.

Sr. Georgine taught with authority. But she was not authoritarian. Authority in the classroom does not mean teaching with an iron fist, a loud voice, or a demanding attitude. Authority is present when we teach in such a way that we permit access to the author of the teachings. Sr. Georgine was the first religion teacher I had that made the Gospel accessible. Her teaching opened doors to the grace of God that previously had seemed elusive. She taught and lived in such a way as to grant me access to the Author whom she preached. From Sr. Georgine, who had such an understanding of life and the Gospel, I've learned to study and reflect on the Gospel and how it pertains to everyday living so that I can lead others to the Author of life.

➕ **Counsel** (right judgment) helps us give advice and also helps us seek advice and be open to the advice of others.

Dad was facing one of the biggest decisions of his life. The building he owned, which housed our apartment and the family drugstore below, was in dire need of repairs. A contractor came out and drew up a proposal for repairs that would require a significant amount of money from my Dad's not-so-deep pockets. Mom and Dad sat at the kitchen table with the contractor, weighing the proposal, as I and my brother Ron (we were the only ones home at the time) looked on. Then my Dad spoke to the contractor,

"Give me a couple of minutes. I want to talk it over with my sons." Dad then took Ron and me, both of college age, into the living room to ask our advice. I was amazed and humbled that the man who had made decisions for his family all his life was now turning to family members for advice. Dad taught me to use the gift of counsel to make right judgments and to help others do the same.

➕ **Fortitude** enables us to stand up for our beliefs, to do what is right in the face of difficulties, and to endure suffering with faith.

Fr. Larry was the chaplain at Cook County Jail. He was taking questions from my students about his ministry when one student asked how many lives he's turned around. Fr. Larry paused and said, "Let's see . . . I've been doing this for fifteen years . . . about five thousand inmates . . . I'd say six. Next question." I called a time out and said, "Whoa, Father, can you explain what keeps you going with a success rate like that?" Without hesitation, he said, "I do it because it's the right thing to do. Jesus said, 'When I was in prison, you visited me.' Next question." I was amazed at this man's fortitude and sense of dedication. Each and every day, without any fanfare, he practiced the Gospel—because it was the right thing to do. I think of the fortitude of Fr. Larry whenever I face a difficult challenge in my ministry or feel as though my "success rate" has taken a beating.

➕ **Knowledge** helps us know what God asks of us and how we should respond.

Regina was the first person I knew who talked about God in a personal way, referring to him as "the Lord." We were in college and I was studying theology. I *knew about* God. But Regina *knew* God. She talked about what the Lord wanted her to do with her life and how she turned to the Lord in prayer when she was faced with some major decisions. Listening to her, I wanted

I'm looking for somewhere to share my gifts.

to know the Lord for myself. In time, I have indeed come to know the Lord. No longer is God a subject in a book to be studied but rather someone to be known. Regina's gift of knowledge inspired me to come to know God and continues to inspire me to help others know God through a life of prayer.

 Fear of the Lord is not about being afraid but of having wonder and awe at the greatness of God and our dependence on him.

I wish I had my mother's eyes. I'm not talking about the color or shape of her eyes, as beautiful as they are. Nor am I talking about her eyesight (mine is actually better). I'm talking about the way she sees the world with the wonder and awe of a child, even after eighty-four years. One day we were making small talk when she said, "Just the other day, I was reading a book and this tiny dot was moving across the page. I thought my eyes were playing tricks on me but then I realized it was the teeniest, tiniest little insect I ever saw. I was thinking about how they say that all of God's creatures have a purpose and I was watching this little fellow crossing the page of my book, wondering what purpose it served in God's creation and realizing that God alone knows!" Now, if I had spotted a bug on the page I probably would've swatted it! Which is precisely why I wish I had my mother's eyes. Somewhere along the way, she learned to recognize God's majesty and she sees it everywhere and "bows" before it. Her fear of the Lord draws her

> **I wish I had my mother's eyes.**

closer to God, not with a casual attitude, but with one of profound respect. From Mom, I've learned and continue to learn how to see with eyes that are like the eyes of a child.

 Piety (reverence) is a gift that helps us love and worship God.

My brother Tom is an avid runner. To raise money for charity, he's run over fifteen marathons. I was surprised to learn that while he runs, he prays the Rosary. He doesn't dangle Rosary beads in front of him while he runs. Rather, he wears a finger Rosary that looks like a simple ring. He wears it on his pinky, and as he runs turns the Rosary ring between thumb and finger. He prays a Hail Mary on each little bump, all the while reflecting on the Lord's Paschal Mystery through the Mysteries of the Rosary. It's a simple and humble piety and not at all conspicuous because it's just a little ring most people wouldn't notice. And yet, Tom shows reverence in this way, worshiping God while doing something as common as running. From Tom, I've learned that piety is an attitude that seeks to praise God in the smallest, humblest, and often most unnoticeable ways.

Present Your Gifts to the Church

A pastor once told me that the local hospital had called, complaining about the Minister of Care who had begun to pay visits to the patients. When the pastor inquired about the person's name, he realized that he had no idea who this person was. It turns out that a young man living in the parish went on a retreat, got all fired up about using his gifts to serve others, and went to the hospital to use his gifts in service of others—without ever letting the parish know! While his desire was very commendable, there are specific ministries that belong to the Church, and the Church reserves the right to discern whether or not an individual indeed possesses the gifts proper to that ministry. Each of us can use our gifts to serve others in our families, at work, and in our communities, as well as in informal ways in our parish community. However, if we seek to use our gifts in parish ministries such as being a catechist, a minister of care, or a liturgical minister, we must present ourselves to the parish and, together with the pastoral staff, discern whether or not we have the *charism* proper to that ministry. Gifts are indeed meant to be shared, but it really helps if we know for sure which gifts we truly have before we try to share them!

Practical suggestions for practicing the Gifts of the Spirit:

> **Wisdom:** strive to avoid judging only by appearance; when encountering a difficult person, look at him or her through the eyes of God; help another person look at a problem from a new perspective—one that reflects how God sees.

> **Understanding:** make a commitment to regular reading, reflection, and study of Catholic literature and sacred Scripture; reflect on your everyday life experiences in light of each day's Scripture readings; commit yourself to making choices within the context of prayer and the reading of Scripture.

> **Counsel (Right Judgment):** offer to help someone else with his or her problems; ask someone for help with a problem or decision that you yourself are facing; bring a decision you are faced with to the Holy Spirit in prayer and ask for guidance.

> **Fortitude:** commit yourself to undertake a challenging task in the service of your faith; continue to offer service to others even when no one notices your efforts; at work or among friends, speak out on a contemporary issue in light of Catholic teaching.

> **Knowledge:** commit yourself to recognizing temptations for what they are; regularly turn to God in prayer in order to know the real value of things; speak to God on an intimate and personal level and ask him to help you know him better.

> **Fear of the Lord:** strive to open your eyes and marvel at God's incredible love for us; take a few moments each day to encounter nature, in good weather and bad, in order to more clearly recognize God's majesty; in your private prayer, bow your head or kneel as a sign of reverence for God's greatness.

> **Piety (Reverence):** try to make your prayerful gestures—bowing, genuflecting, making the Sign of the Cross—with reverence and not casually; include humble acts of piety in your daily activities such as making the Sign of the Cross before a meal in a public place or praying a Rosary or the Liturgy of the Hours while traveling by train, bus, or plane; show reverence to others.

Scripture

A shoot shall come out from the stock of Jesse, and a branch shall grow out of his roots. The spirit of the LORD shall rest on him, the spirit of wisdom and understanding, the spirit of counsel and might, the spirit of knowledge and the fear of the LORD. (ISAIAH 11:1–2)

Prayer

Holy Spirit, thank you for generously sharing yourself and your gifts with me. Show me how to use these gifts in service to others. Inspire me to recognize your gifts within me and to show gratitude for them always. Fill me with a spirit of wisdom and understanding, the spirit of right judgment and courage, the spirit of knowledge and reverence, and the spirit of wonder and awe in your presence. Amen.

To share and learn more in a spiritual mentoring relationship about practicing the Gifts of the Spirit, visit www.loyolapress.com/practice-makes-catholic.

Practice 8

Pray with the Whole Church

"We believe in the communion of all the faithful of Christ, those who are pilgrims on earth, the dead who are being purified, and the blessed in heaven, all together forming one Church; and we believe that in this communion, the merciful love of God and his saints is always [attentive] to our prayers" (Paul VI, *The Credo of the People of God*, 30)

"They're Here!"

A famous scene from Steven Spielberg's 1982 movie *Poltergeist* shows little Carol Anne Freeling (played by the late Heather O'Rourke) with her hands pressed up against a TV screen filled with nothing but white noise as she says in a little singsong voice, "They're here!" The not-so-subtle message is that she has made contact with seemingly benign but soon-to-be vicious ghosts.

Supernatural horror films often play upon a common human fear or suspicion that we are not alone in this universe! Whether they be ghosts, goblins, or extraterrestrials, it seems that we are obsessed with the notion of communicating with the great beyond.

For Catholics, the notion that we are not alone in this universe is nothing new, nor is it at all scary. We believe that God is the creator of all things visible and invisible, and that the invisible includes those who have died. They are not gone; they are still with us, but in a different way. We are separated from them by a veil between this life and the afterlife. But we believe without a doubt that, "they're here!"

The Communion of Saints

A few years ago, a number of family members decided to go to a Chicago Blackhawks hockey game. My mom, age eighty-one at the time, also came along. I was concerned that the evening might be too much for her—we would spend several noisy hours in the cold and the crowd. I kept an eye on her throughout the game as she cheered for the Hawks. When the game went into overtime and then finally a shootout, I looked over and noticed that Mom had her face buried in her hands. I asked if she was OK and she gave a slight smile and said she was fine. The Hawks won the shootout, and as we walked back to the car celebrating their victory, Mom went on about how exciting the evening had been. Then she leaned over to me and said, "And when I had my head down before, I was talking to Dad. I said, 'John, this one's for you!'" It made perfect sense for my Mom to talk to Dad at a Hawks game because the two of them used to take the streetcar to watch the Hawks at the old Chicago Stadium when they were dating back in the day. Mom understood that, through the communion of saints, she and Dad could still enjoy a good hockey game together!

> For Catholics, the notion that we are not alone in this universe is nothing new, nor is it at all scary.

Our Catholic commitment to community is so strong, that even death cannot separate us from one another. We know that we continue to be connected in a special way to those who have died in Christ Jesus. Because of the immortality of the soul, we believe that we can and do remain in communication with deceased faithful followers of Christ through the *communion of saints*. The communion of saints is made up of, not only canonized (official) saints, but of all those faithful followers of Jesus who have passed from this life to the next: parents, grandparents,

> "The saints are the sinners who keep on going."
> ROBERT LOUIS STEVENSON

Patron Saints

Catholics turn to specific saints, asking for their intercession in certain situations. We refer to these as patron saints, meaning that, because of how they lived, these saints have been designated as appropriate intercessors on behalf of countries, professions, activities, situations, and so on. A saint is named as a patron because of some relationship between his or her life and the particular cause being prayed for. Here are a few famous patron saints and their causes:

> St. Jude: lost causes
> St. Anthony: lost items
> St. Francis of Assisi: animals
> St. Peregrine: people suffering from cancer
> St. Isidore: farmers
> St. Thomas More: lawyers
> St. Dymphna: people suffering from mental illness
> St. Agatha: nurses
> St. Michael the Archangel: police officers
> St. Cecilia: singers
> St. Joseph: workers

aunts, uncles, children, cousins, friends, neighbors, and so on. Through their prayers and intercession, we can be helped. By the same token, through our prayers, the souls in purgatory can find assistance.

A few more words about the souls "in" purgatory. As I described in my book, *A Well-Built Faith*, purgatory is not a place but is a state of transition and purification for those who die in the love of God but who have not fully let go of whatever separates them from that love. Before we enter God's presence in heaven, we must be cleansed of every trace of sin. This cleansing is thought of as painful in the same way that moving from a dark room into bright sunlight can hurt our eyes until they adjust. For this reason, and since the earliest days of the Church, Catholics pray for those who have died, to ease their transition.

A Very Special Connection: Mary

Among all the saints, Mary, the Mother of Jesus, is a very special connection. Because of her unique relationship with Jesus, we can go to her for help in growing closer to Jesus. We do not worship Mary, nor do we pray to her. Rather, we honor her and we pray in communion with her, knowing that, through her we can come to know her son, Jesus. Think of it this way. When people are hoping to meet that special someone, it's not unusual for them to ask for help. Maybe a friend can introduce you to the person you are trying to get to know. Maybe this friend can give you some insight into what this person is like. It helps to have connections. Mary is that very special connection for us. Through her, we can grow closer to her son, Jesus. Prayer that involves Mary and the saints is called *intercessory* prayer—Mary and the saints *intercede* on our behalf, meaning that they pray for us and with us.

> Among all the saints, Mary, the Mother of Jesus is a very special connection.

The most well-known Marian prayer is, of course, the Hail Mary. The first part of this prayer recalls the words that the angel Gabriel spoke to Mary at the Annunciation:

"Greetings, favoured one! The Lord is with you." (Luke 1:28)

as well as the words that Elizabeth spoke to Mary at the Visitation:

> "Blessed are you among women, and blessed is the fruit of your womb." (Luke 1:42)

Jesus was walking along one day, when He came upon a group of people surrounding a lady of ill repute. It was obvious that the crowd was preparing to stone her, so Jesus made His now-famous statement, "Let the person who has no sin cast the first stone." The crowd was shamed and one by one began to turn away. All of a sudden, a lovely little woman made her way through the crowd. Finally getting to the front, the woman sheepishly tossed a pebble towards the woman. Jesus looked over and said, "I really hate it when you do that, Mom."

The second part of the prayer is simply our request for Mary to pray for us:

"Holy Mary, Mother of God, pray for us sinners, now and at the hour of our death. Amen."

In all, Marian prayers, such as the Hail Mary, point to Jesus, honor Mary, and ask for her intercession. Another Marian prayer that exemplifies this is the Litany of the Blessed

"Harry, some people out here want to know if they can have a room.

Virgin Mary. This litany begins by praising the Trinity and then flows with dozens of rich, poetic images that honor Mary. Each invocation is followed by the response "pray for us." Here is a sampling of some of these beautiful invocations from the Litany of the Blessed Virgin Mary:

- ✚ **Mirror of justice**
- ✚ **Seat of wisdom**
- ✚ **Cause of our joy**
- ✚ **Mystical rose**
- ✚ **Gate of Heaven**

- ✚ **Morning star**
- ✚ **Health of the sick**
- ✚ **Refuge of sinners**
- ✚ **Comforter of the afflicted**
- ✚ **Help of Christians**

You've Got the Network

A well-known advertising campaign for a wireless cell phone company often depicts someone using their phone while backed up by an army of people who are there to assist, assuring customers that they are supported by a reliable network. Well, we are backed by a network of those who "have gone before us with the sign of faith and rest in the sleep of peace." (Eucharistic Prayer I, *The Roman Missal*) We are not alone. The communion of saints, with Mary at the forefront, are with us wherever we go, ready to assist us in finding our way to Jesus.

May Crowning

One popular devotion that honors Mary during the month of May (a month devoted to honoring the Blessed Virgin) is the May crowning. This beautiful devotion traditionally involves processions, flowers, Marian hymns, and children dressed in their finest (the girls wearing white dresses). You can celebrate a simple May crowning with your family or with any group of friends, neighbors, or fellow parishioners by including the following elements:

> Place a statue of Mary on a pedestal.

> Sing a hymn honoring Mary.

> Read a Scripture passage about Mary such as Luke 1:26-38 (the Annunciation); Luke 1:39-45 (the Visitation); Luke 2:6-12 (the Nativity); Luke 2:41-50 (the boy Jesus in the Temple); John 2:1-12 (the wedding feast at Cana); Luke 23:27-29 (Mary meets Jesus carrying his cross); John 19:25-30 (Mary at the foot of the cross).

> Offer a brief reflection on the role of Mary as the first disciple.

> Walk in procession while singing or playing a Marian hymn.

> Place a garland of flowers on the head of the statue.

> Pray the Hail Mary, the Hail, Holy Queen, or the Memorare.

Practical suggestions for practicing praying with Mary and with/for the communion of saints and the souls in purgatory:

> Get to know your own patron saint better (by reading and studying the Lives of the Saints) and then seek the intercession of your patron on a regular basis.

> Look up your patron saint's feast day (see http://saints.sqpn.com/indexsnt.htm) and commemorate this day in a special way.

> If you were not named after a saint (and did not choose a saint's name for Confirmation), feel free to choose a saint to become your patron. In a sense, you can "adopt" a saint as your patron.

> Find a holy card, icon, statue, or other sacred image of your patron saint and place it in a prominent location in your home or place of work as a reminder of your patron's constant assistance.

> Pray regularly for those special people in your life who have died. Pray for them and ask them for their intercession, knowing that their immortal souls live on and that, through the communion of saints, we are still connected with them.

> Learn the traditional prayer for the deceased: "Eternal rest, grant unto them, O Lord, and let perpetual light shine upon them. May their souls and the souls of all the faithful departed, through the mercy of God, rest in peace. Amen."

> Honor Mary by observing all her special feast days in the Church's liturgical calendar. For a complete list, visit http://campus.udayton.edu/mary/resources/dogmas.html.

> Pray the Rosary as a way of growing closer to Jesus through Mary (see practice 1 of this book).

> Learn the Church's Marian prayers: the Hail Mary, the Memorare, the Hail, Holy Queen (Regina Coeli), the Magnificat, and the Litany of the Blessed Virgin Mary, just to name a few.

Scripture

In those days Mary set out and went with haste to a Judean town in the hill country, where she entered the house of Zechariah and greeted Elizabeth. When Elizabeth heard Mary's greeting, the child leapt in her womb. And Elizabeth was filled with the Holy Spirit and exclaimed with a loud cry, "Blessed are you among women, and blessed is the fruit of your womb." (LUKE 1:39–42)

Prayer

Hail Mary, full of grace, the Lord is with you. Blessed are you among women and blessed is the fruit of your womb, Jesus. Holy Mary, Mother of God, pray for (*add the names of those you wish to pray for* _____) and for all of us sinners, now and at the hour of our death. Amen.

(Think of those who have died)

Eternal rest, grant unto them, O Lord, and let perpetual light shine upon them. (3x)

May their souls and the souls of all the faithful departed, through the mercy of God, rest in peace. Amen.

To share and learn more in a spiritual mentoring relationship about practicing praying with Mary, the communion of saints, and for the souls in purgatory, visit www.loyolapress.com/practice-makes-catholic.

Practice 9

Welcome One Another

We call upon all people of good will, but Catholics especially, to welcome the newcomers in their neighborhoods and schools, in their places of work and worship, with heartfelt hospitality, openness, and eagerness both to help and to learn from our brothers and sisters, of whatever race, religion, ethnicity, or background. (*Welcoming the Stranger Among Us: Unity in Diversity, A Statement of the U.S. Catholic Bishops*, 2000)

Wal-Mart Did Not Invent Hospitality

Let's face it, most of us like to be fawned over! Especially when we go to a nice restaurant or an upscale hotel. We appreciate it when the service at such establishments communicates a high regard for our well-being. We usually reward outstanding service with a generous tip; it's our way of showing how much we appreciate their hospitality.

Today, hospitality is big business. Wal-Mart in particular is well-known for its greeters who welcome you into their stores. But hospitality is much more than a business strategy—it is at the very core of human relationships. In fact, in biblical times, hospitality was considered one's duty. A person took his life in his hands by traveling the dangerous roads of the remote regions in the Middle East. If a traveler showed up at your home, you saved his life by offering hospitality. By offering food, water, and safe lodging, you enabled the traveler to live another day and continue his journey.

Today, in most cases, traveling is not quite that dramatic. And yet, the notion of hospitality as a core human gesture remains—it is a way of recognizing and reaffirming our common bond as children of God. This bond is deepened in a profound way through the sacraments of initiation (baptism, confirmation, and eucharist). As members of the Body of Christ, we share a bond with our Christian brothers and sisters. This does not mean that our hospitality is limited to fellow Catholics. The community we experience within the Church is a sign of the community that all humanity is called to share in. By extending hospitality to all those we meet, we express in profound and yet simple ways the very Catholic notion of community.

In biblical times, hospitality was considered one's duty.

In his book, *Easter Gospels* (Minneapolis, MN: Augsburg, 1983), R. H. Smith explains that hospitality plays a crucial role in the story of the two disciples on the road to Emmaus (Luke 24:13–35). After walking the road and talking with a stranger about the catastrophic events of the Crucifixion, the two disciples extend hospitality to the stranger who has joined them on the road. As a result of their act of hospitality, the stranger reveals himself in the breaking of the bread as the risen Christ. Smith writes: "So the lordship of Jesus is not known or manifested in acts of war or vengeance or in dreadful and mighty signs, but is attained through a cross and expressed in a meal—an act of hospitality, peace, brotherhood, and sisterhood." Through our own acts of hospitality, we too can come to recognize the risen Christ in our midst.

"Esther has the gift of hospitality."

A priest was assigned to a parish in a dry county (one that forbids the sale of alcohol). One day, he went to visit one of his parishioners only to discover that the man was bootlegging peach brandy. The man said that he would come to Mass if the priest would drink some of his brandy and admit doing so during his homily. The priest agreed and had a drink. That Sunday at Mass, the priest recognized the man sitting in the congregation. During his homily, he said, "I'd like to welcome Mr. Johnson to our parish community and thank him for the hospitality he extended to me earlier this week when I visited him, especially for the peaches he gave me and the spirit in which they were given."

A closer look at Matthew 25:34–35 teaches us that hospitality is not merely the frosting on the cake; it is an essential ingredient in the recipe we call discipleship:

> Then the king will say to those at his right hand, "Come, you that are blessed by my Father, inherit the kingdom prepared for you from the foundation of the world; for I was hungry and you gave me food, I was thirsty and you gave me something to drink, I was a stranger and you welcomed me."

Hospitality and Evangelization

Hospitality is so important to our identity as Catholics that the U. S. Conference of Catholic Bishops identified it as one of three goals in their evangelization plan titled *Go and Make Disciples*:

> Goal II: To invite all people in the United States, whatever their social or cultural background, to hear the message of salvation in Jesus Christ so they may come to join us in the fullness of the Catholic faith.

In describing this goal, the bishops go on to say:

> This goal means not only that people are invited but also that an essential welcoming spirit is present in Catholic homes and in all our Catholic institutions: parishes, organizations, hospitals, schools, chanceries, and centers of neighborhood service.

Ministry of Hospitality

It is not uncommon today to enter a Catholic Church on Sunday and to be welcomed at the door by a greeter—a minister of hospitality. Such greeters are true liturgical ministers since they echo St. Paul's instructions to "welcome one another, therefore, just as Christ has welcomed you" (Romans 15:7). These ministers are not simply creating some kind of "touchy-feely, feel-good experience." Rather, they help to form us into the Body of Christ that we become as a result of the celebration of the Eucharist. Their simple acts of hospitality serve to remind us that we are gathering for a communal action; the Eucharist is not a private action. We, in turn, then, are called to share this same hospitality with those we encounter as we enter the Church and find our seat. We can thank ministers of hospitality for taking the first steps to gather us together as the Body of Christ.

The strategy behind this goal is to create a more welcoming attitude toward others in our parishes so that people feel at home; next, to create an attitude of sharing faith and to develop greater skills to do this; then, to undertake activities to invite others to know the Catholic people better. (104–105)

Practical suggestions for practicing hospitality:

> Start in your own home. Recommit yourself to extending hospitality to the people you live with and interact with on an everyday basis. Seek nothing in return, but offer it as an expression of community.

> Volunteer at your parish to become a minister of hospitality (or to begin such a ministry). Know that sincerely welcoming people to church as they arrive is an expression of the church's deep appreciation for their presence and for their membership in the Body of Christ.

> Extend hospitality as you travel to and from work each day. Instead of trying to be first in line for the train or grabbing the last seat on the bus, step aside and offer the opportunity to someone else. Do the same when driving your car. Instead of seeking to outrun everyone else, practice defensive driving and drive with a sense of hospitality, allowing people to move ahead of you or to turn before you.

> Occasionally take snacks or treats to your place of work and share them with others for no other reason than to express hospitality.

> Invite a friend or neighbor out for a bite to eat or to your home for some tea or coffee (or a beer or a glass of wine as the case may be) for a chance to visit and chat for a while.

> If you'd like to be involved in a parish ministry such as the RCIA or adult catechesis, but don't feel that you have the gift of serving as a catechist, volunteer to be the minister of hospitality for that group on a regular basis, coordinating the refreshments for each gathering and seeing to it that all the participants are well taken care of before, during, and after the gatherings.

> Stay informed about immigration issues; help your community (and nation) work toward a just immigration policy that is driven by a welcoming spirit of hospitality.

> **"There is an emanation from the heart in genuine hospitality which cannot be described, but is immediately felt and puts the stranger at once at his ease."**
> Washington Irving

Scripture

"Let mutual love continue. Do not neglect to show hospitality to strangers, for by doing that some have entertained angels without knowing it."
(HEBREWS 13:1–2)

Prayer

Lord, Jesus, you welcomed me into your loving embrace in baptism and have welcomed me back into your arms each time that I have sinned and repented. May I learn to be welcoming to others, extending hospitality to all those I encounter so that they will recognize your abundant love. May I build up the Body of Christ through the hospitality I offer to others. Help me recognize all people as my brothers and sisters. Amen.

To share and learn more in a spiritual mentoring relationship about practicing hospitality, visit www.loyolapress.com/practice-makes-catholic.

PART THREE

A RESPECT FOR HUMAN LIFE

I n the television classic *A Charlie Brown Christmas*, Pigpen has been assigned the role of the innkeeper for the Christmas nativity pageant. Unfortunately for him, the innkeeper's wife is played by Frieda who complains that all of Pigpen's dust is ruining her naturally curly hair. Charlie Brown suggests that Frieda not look at it as dust but as soil from some ancient civilization, possibly trod upon by Solomon or even Nebuchadnezzar. In other words, Charlie tries to restore Pigpen's dignity. Immediately Pigpen looks at Frieda and says, "Sort of makes you want to treat me with more respect, doesn't it?"

Dignity and respect go hand in hand. Catholics respect the dignity of every human life, from the moment of conception to the moment of death and beyond. We are committed to working for justice, seeking to build structures and practices in society that respect the dignity of human beings and eliminating those structures and practices that do not.

In part 3, we'll look at the following Catholic practices related to respect for the dignity of human life and a commitment to justice:

Practice 10: Show Mercy

Practice 11: Do Justice and Live Virtuously

Practice 12: Work for the Common Good

Practice 13: Keep the Ten Commandments

To share and learn more in a mentoring relationship about practicing Catholic respect for the dignity of human life and a commitment to justice, visit www.loyolapress.com/practice-makes-catholic.

Practice 10

Show Mercy

Man attains to the merciful love of God, His mercy, to the extent that he himself is interiorly transformed in the spirit of that love towards his neighbor. (Pope John Paul II, *Rich in Mercy*, 14)

Mister Cellophane

In the musical *Chicago*, there's a lovable but pathetic character named Amos, the rather thick-skulled husband of accused murderer Roxie Hart. Throughout the story, poor Amos is dismissed by everyone as being inconsequential and unimportant. Despite his best efforts, he is ignored and goes unnoticed by everyone, most notably by his wife Roxie and her lawyer Billy Flynn. At one point in the musical, Amos launches into a song in which he laments:

> Cellophane,
> Mister Cellophane,
> Should have been my name,
> Mister Cellophane,
> 'Cause you can look right through me,
> Walk right by me,
> And never know I'm there!

Unfortunately, there a lot of people in the world who feel this way. You and I can go through our lives day in and day out and never notice that some people are in need and deserving of attention. This is the essence of Jesus' story of the Rich Man and Lazarus (Luke 16:19–31): the rich man is condemned, not for what he has done, but for what he has failed to do—he has failed to recognize the hunger and poverty of the man at his gate, Lazarus.

Jesus revisits this notion of not recognizing the needs of others in the Parable of the Last Judgment (Matthew 25:44–46).

> Then they also will answer, "Lord, when was it that we saw you hungry or thirsty or a stranger or naked or sick or in prison, and did not take care of you?" Then he will answer them, "Truly I tell you, just as you did not do it to one of the least of these, you did not do it to me." And these will go away into eternal punishment, but the righteous into eternal life.

Jesus is warning us that, unless we adjust our vision, we risk looking right through and walking right by our neighbors in need, not recognizing their dignity as children of God. Jesus is alerting us to the danger of sins of omission. To remedy this situation, the church provides us with the corporal works of mercy, which are based on that parable of the Last Judgment.

You and I can go through our lives day in and day out and never notice that some people are in need and deserving of attention.

➕ **Feed the Hungry**–it is estimated that over 1 billion people in the world go hungry each day (Bread for the World Institute).

➕ **Shelter the Homeless**–approximately 3.5 million people, 1.35 million of them children, experience homelessness in a given year in the U.S. (National Law Center on Homelessness and Poverty).

➕ **Clothe the Naked**–more than 28 million children living in low-income families in the U.S. are in need of clothing (The Salvation Army).

➕ **Visit the Sick**–by the year 2020, about 157 million Americans will be afflicted with some type of chronic illness (U.S. Department of Health and Human Services).

- **Visit the Imprisoned**—1.6 million people are serving sentences in U.S. state and federal prisons, and another 785,000 are serving sentences in local jails (U.S. Department of Justice).

- **Give to the Poor**—nearly 40 million people, including nearly 13 million children, live below the poverty line in the U.S. (U.S. Census Bureau).

- **Bury the Dead**—last I checked, no ordinary human being has yet to escape death!

The corporal works of mercy are kind acts by which we help our neighbors with their everyday material and physical needs. The key to these works of mercy is that they are not the sorts of actions that happen by accident. In order for them to happen, we need to be proactive. When we think about what we are to do as followers of Jesus, the Corporal Works of Mercy can act as guides for our actions. These works remind us that our Catholic faith is to be put into action. We cannot say that we love God and then ignore the needs of our neighbors. The Corporal Works of Mercy are not abstract qualities: they are concrete actions that Jesus himself spoke of.

Where Did "Bury the Dead" Come From?

If you've been looking through Matthew 25, trying to find reference to "bury the dead" as one of the corporal works of mercy, you've no doubt come up empty. This work of mercy was added by the third century, a time when the Christian community was forced to recover the bodies of martyrs that had been discarded in the streets or left in gruesome public display. This work echoes Tobit 1:17-19, which reveals that, for the Jewish people, deprivation of burial was considered a horrific offense. Adding this Work of Mercy rounds out to the number seven, a number that symbolizes perfection in the Bible. Finally, this work of mercy emphasizes that "even death cannot rob us of our fundamental dignity as human persons." (*Reflections on the Body, Cremation and Catholic Burial Rites*, 1998, U.S. Catholic Bishops)

Deciding that he wanted to meet God and figuring that it might be a long trip to where God lived, a little boy packed his backpack with brownies and some juice boxes and was on his way. A few blocks away from home, the boy stopped to rest, sitting down next to an elderly man who was feeding the pigeons. The boy was about to snack on his brownies and juice boxes when he noticed that the man looked hungry and thirsty, so he offered them to him. The man gratefully accepted and smiled at the boy with the most beautiful smile the boy had ever seen. The two sat there all afternoon eating and smiling, without speaking a word. Finally, feeling a bit sleepy, the boy decided to head home, but not before giving the old man a hug. When the boy reached home and his mom asked why he looked so happy, he replied, "I had lunch with God. You know what? God's got the most beautiful smile I've ever seen." Meanwhile, when the elderly man returned home and his son asked why he looked so happy, the old man said, "I ate brownies and drank juice boxes in the park with God. You know, he's much younger than I expected."

Corporal: Let's Get Physical

As a kid, I thought that the corporal works of mercy had something to do with the military—corporals, sergeants, generals. Of course, the word *corporal*, when referring to the works of mercy, is derived from the Latin word *corpus*, which means "of the body" or "physical." Thus, the corporal works of mercy are actions that flow from our Catholic understanding of the human body. Catholics are not dualists; we do not believe that the human body and human soul are distinct realities at war with each

> **The Corporal Works of Mercy are not mere sentimentality.**

other. We believe that the two are intimately connected, inseparable in this earthly life. According to the *Catechism of the Catholic Church*:

> Man, though made of body and soul, is a unity. For this reason man may not despise his bodily life. Rather he is obliged to regard his body as good and to hold it in honor since God has created it and will raise it up on the last day. (364)

We hold the human body in honor, recognizing that life and physical health are gifts from God. This means that we not only pay attention to our own physical needs, but, because of our commitment to community, to the physical needs of others. The corporal works of mercy are not mere sentimentality. They are actions that spread hope and proclaim the Gospel; they evangelize without words. They are actions through which we share in the suffering of others, the true meaning of the word *consolation*.

"Christians must make tough choices. Voting to send our roofing fund to famine victims was one of those."

Mercy!

In essence, *mercy* is an action that gives evidence of divine favor—a blessing. One of the most famous utterances of the word *mercy* is from the classic Roy Orbison song "Pretty Woman"—expressing his sentiment that this "pretty woman walking down the street" was enough evidence for him that there is a God! By the way, that pretty woman was Roy Orbison's wife, Claudette, who inspired the song. Mercy is an action that reveals God's presence because God is merciful (generous in showering his blessings on us). It makes perfect sense, then, to refer to these charitable actions—feeding the hungry, visiting the sick and imprisoned, clothing the naked, and so on—as works of mercy since they reveal God's presence.

> **"This is the spirit of the Order, indeed the true spirit of Mercy flowing on us."**
> CATHERINE MCAULEY, FOUNDRESS OF THE SISTERS OF MERCY

When we perform the corporal works of mercy, we are not doing so to earn grace, please God, or draw attention to our own holiness. We do so to

But Isn't the Church Opposed to the Body?

All too often, society concludes that Christianity—the Catholic Church in particular—is opposed to the body. Granted, there have been strains of anti-body sentiment in Church teaching over the centuries. Much of that comes from a misreading of St. Paul when he says things such as "To set the mind on the flesh is death, but to set the mind on the Spirit is life and peace" (Romans 8:6). When St. Paul speaks of "the flesh," which he often condemns, he is not speaking of the human body but of life devoid of the Holy Spirit. Actually, the Catholic Church is very pro-body. In particular, Pope John Paul II is credited with articulating a theology of the body during his pontificate that presents a vision of the human person that is integrated: body, soul, and spirit.

reveal God's presence to others and as an act of stewardship, to respond to the overflow of grace that we ourselves have received. In fact, most Catholics are more comfortable evangelizing through works of mercy than through words. As a sacramental people, we express ourselves beyond words, relying on actions and gestures. The corporal works of mercy are actions and gestures that reveal God's love and express our love for God and neighbor.

Practical suggestions for practicing the corporal works of mercy:

> **Feed the Hungry**—see to the proper nutrition of your own children, support and volunteer for food pantries, soup kitchens, and agencies that feed the hungry; make a few sandwiches to hand out as you walk through areas where you might encounter people in need; educate yourself about world hunger; avoid wasting food; share your meals with others.

> **Shelter the Homeless**—help neighbors care for their homes and do repairs; support and/or volunteer at a homeless shelter; support and/or volunteer for charitable agencies who care for the homeless, build homes, and provide support in the wake of natural disasters; advocate for public policies and legislation that provide housing for low-income people; consider becoming a foster parent.

> **Clothe the Naked**—go through your drawers and closets and find good-condition clothes and shoes to donate to agencies that provide assistance for those in need; participate in programs that provide towels and linens for hospitals in distressed areas.

> **Visit the Sick**—spend quality time with those who are sick or home-bound; take the time to call, send a card or an e-mail to someone who is sick; volunteer to drive patients to medical appointments and treatment facilities; volunteer at a hospital; assist those who are full-time caregivers for family members; cook and deliver meals to the sick and homebound.

> **Visit the Imprisoned**—support and/or participate in ministries to those who are incarcerated; support programs sponsored by agencies that advocate on behalf of those who are unjustly imprisoned; support job-training and educational programs designed to rehabilitate prisoners; pray for the families of inmates; support programs that provide holiday gifts for prisoners and their families; support efforts that seek the abolition of the death penalty.

> **Give to the Poor**—take some small bills or loose change (or coupon books if you prefer not to carry cash) with you to hand out to people you encounter who are in need; throw your coin change into a jar and periodically donate it to a charity; if possible make a regular monetary donation to a charity that tends to the needs of the poor.

> **Bury the Dead**—be faithful about attending wakes/visitation; support or volunteer at a hospice; participate in a bereavement ministry; spend time with widows and widowers; take friends and relatives to visit the cemetery; support ministries that offer free Christian burials to those unable to afford one; offer daily prayers for those with terminal illnesses and for those who have died; send Mass cards to families of those who have died.

Scripture

"For I was hungry and you gave me food, I was thirsty and you gave me something to drink, I was a stranger and you welcomed me, I was naked and you gave me clothing, I was sick and you took care of me, I was in prison and you visited to me." (Matthew 25:35–36)

Prayer

Lord, God, I pray that you open my eyes to help me recognize the needs of others. Help me see more clearly than the rich man who did not notice poor Lazarus at his gate. Fill me with a generous heart so that I may perform the corporal works of mercy, tending to the physical needs of my brothers and sisters in this world. May I do so, not for attention or to earn your grace, but to reveal your rich and compassionate mercy—the same mercy you have shown to me time and again. Amen.

To share and learn more in a spiritual mentoring relationship about practicing the corporal works of mercy, visit www.loyolapress.com/practice-makes-catholic.

Practice 11

Do Justice and Live Virtuously

Human virtues acquired by education, by deliberate acts and by a perseverance ever-renewed in repeated efforts are purified and elevated by divine grace. With God's help, they forge character and give facility in the practice of the good. (*Catechism of the Catholic Church*, 1810)

Habits You Don't Want to Break

We all have bad habits. Perhaps we talk with our mouth full, frequently use an annoying phrase, forget to pick up after ourselves, or, in a more serious vein, smoke cigarettes. Kicking such bad habits can improve relationships and, in the case of smoking, improve our very health.

On the other hand, not all habits are bad. In the 1980s, a very popular book, *The Seven Habits of Highly Effective People* by Stephen Covey, focused on seven principles or habits for success. While Covey's idea was a brilliant approach to solving personal and professional problems, the concept was not unique. For centuries, the Church has taught seven habits or principles that are key to living as a disciple of Jesus. These habits are called virtues. We can refer to them as habits because they need to be used; they can be lost if they are neglected. As followers of Jesus, we can carry out our mission effectively if we rely on the following habits, or virtues.

The first three virtues are called theological virtues because they come from God and lead to God. (We will deal with the practice of these three virtues in a later chapter.)

✚ **Faith**—is the ability to believe in God and give our lives to him.

✚ **Hope**—is the desire for all the good things God has planned for us.

✚ **Charity**—is the desire to love God above all things and our neighbor as ourselves.

The remaining four virtues, which are the focus of this chapter, are called the *cardinal* virtues (from the Latin word for "hinge" (*cardo*), meaning "that on which other things depend."

✚ **Prudence**—is the ability to decide what is good and then choose to do it.

✚ **Justice**—is respect for the rights of others and the desire to give them what is rightfully theirs.

✚ **Fortitude**—is the courage to do what is right even when it is very difficult.

✚ **Temperance**—is the ability to balance what we want with what we need.

These are not the only virtues, but they are the foundation upon which all other virtues rest. The cardinal virtues are human virtues, acquired by education and good actions. Like playing the piano, being a good friend, playing sports, or anything else worthwhile, these virtues take time and effort to develop. But through practice they can become a natural part of our lives.

It is not uncommon to hear people lament the lack of civility and respect that people show for one another in our society today. By practicing the virtues, we can offer an alternative, a way of behaving that is grounded in respect for ourselves and others.

Prudence

One of the most famous questions asked on late-night television was on *The Tonight Show* in 1995, when Jay Leno interviewed actor Hugh Grant, not long after Grant had been arrested for seeing a prostitute. To the roar of audience laughter, Leno bluntly asked, "What were you thinking?" Most of us would agree that Mr. Grant had not been thinking at all! Many of us have been on the receiving end of this question, most likely from our parents, after we had done something stupid. Prudence is the habit of thinking before acting. This flies in the face of today's mentality of "Just do it!" While there is something to be said for spontaneity, some of our choices in life require deep thought, prayer, and consideration, lest we find ourselves facing the consequences of a poor decision. That's where prudence comes in.

St. Ignatius of Loyola used the word *discernment* to describe the process of making a decision based on prudence. To make a decision with prudence is to honor the place of God's will in our lives. It is an interior search that seeks to align our own will with the will of God so that we can learn what God is calling us to do and become. Every choice we make, no matter how small, is an opportunity to be prudent.

> **"The power of a man's virtue should not be measured by his special efforts, but by his ordinary doing."**
> BLAISE PASCAL

"We can't just throw our junk away! Why, some missionary church would <u>love</u> to have our junk!"

Tips for Practicing Prudence

Here are some tried-and-true pointers that can help you be prudent and discern God's will.

> Talk to someone you respect.

> Find some solitude.

> Start with what you know.

> Tell God what you desire and what you fear.

> Let God speak to you.

> Know that God has a plan for you and pray to follow his will.

> Be patient.

> Prayerfully commit to your decision

> Check out the fruits of your decision.

Relying on prudence in the discernment process can help you when you face decisions. Even though making good decisions can be difficult at times, trust that the Holy Spirit is with you to guide you and help you choose the prudent way.

Justice

"I demand justice!" When people use this phrase, what they often mean is "I want revenge!" The Bible, however, understands justice as much more than this. While Scripture tells us that God does bring retribution on those who do wrong, we also find God expressing justice through his faithfulness, trustworthiness, and compassion. To say that God is just means that you can always count on him to do the right thing—to show compassion and mercy in all situations.

With this understanding, the people of Israel prayed for God's justice, meaning that they prayed that God would stand by them and do the right thing, being compassionate and merciful toward them. The people, in turn, recognized that God expected them to deal with one another in the same way, namely by respecting people's rights, by fulfilling their obligations to one another, by showing compassion and mercy to others in all situations, and by caring for those in need of any kind. For example, the Old Testament teaching about "an eye for an eye and a tooth for a tooth" (Exodus 21:24) was not intended to promote revenge but sought to ensure that punishment would be equal to the crime and not become an excuse for excessive revenge.

With this understanding of justice, we realize that God's call to be just means a summons to practice justice in every aspect of daily life. In essence, to live justly is to live in right relationship with God and neighbor. Anything that separates us from God and from one another is unjust.

At times, we are able to provide direct aid to people in need. These are works of charity and mercy. At other times, we are called to challenge the structures that create and perpetuate these needs. This is called social justice. We'll deal with this concept a little later in this chapter.

Fortitude

I've often thought that the Winter Olympics are rather peculiar. Don't get me wrong, I love to watch them, but it seems as though many of the events are not so much sports as they are dares. The giant slalom, bobsledding, skeleton, ski jumping, snowboard cross, halfpipe, and so on. The athletes who participate in these events are very daring individuals.

Daring is not to be confused with the virtue of fortitude. A daring person is willing to take risks, to be bold and adventurous, bordering on reckless. Fortitude is not recklessness; it is the courage needed to endure uncertainty, danger, intimidation, and even pain for the sake of what is right and good.

I rely on fortitude to perform my role as a public speaker. I'm actually an introvert, more comfortable in situations where I am alone and do not have to talk.

> ## Do Not Be Afraid
>
> It is no coincidence that one of the most oft-repeated lines in the Bible is the phrase, "Do not be afraid" or some variation thereof such as:
>
> > Do not fear
> > Fear not.
> > Have no fear.
> > Be not afraid.
> > Do not be fainthearted.
> > Do not lose heart.
> > Do not give way to fear.
> > Peace be with you.
>
> God makes it clear, throughout the Bible, that we need to practice the virtue of fortitude, knowing that with God's grace, anything and everything can be overcome!

However, God has called me to be a teacher and a public speaker. By practicing the virtue of fortitude (and by relying on the Gift of the Holy Spirit that is also called fortitude), I am able to overcome my fears and speak to groups of all sizes—from two or three to over a thousand! Fortitude helps us moderate fear and overcome obstacles.

Temperance

My favorite pig-out food is pizza! When it comes to pizza, my eyes grow ten times larger than my stomach. Many a time I have indulged in pizza—whether thin crust, thick crust, pan, or deep dish—until I've needed to loosen my belt. My stomach can be screaming, "I'm full!" but my eyes are saying, "more!"

At such times, I could stand to practice a little temperance, a virtue that enables us to practice moderation. And we're not just talking about food. Temperance is a virtue that brings moderation to our natural appetite for pleasures of the senses: eating, drinking, sexual activity, and the like. Temperance does not seek to squelch enjoyment but rather to guard against excess. Too much of a good thing can throw our lives out of balance. When we practice temperance, we are able to maintain balance.

Temperance can further be broken down into several subcategories. One of these is modesty, which guards how we present ourselves to others, especially in the way we dress. Modesty, not to be confused with prudishness, seeks to guard that which is intimate, "refusing to unveil what should remain hidden." (*Catechism of the Catholic Church*, 2521). Another subcategory of temperance is chastity, which is the moderation of one's sexual desires. Finally, temperance also can be applied to economic matters, helping us to moderate our desires for material goods.

A Jesuit and a Franciscan sat down to dinner and a pie was served for dessert. There were two slices, one very small and one very large. The Jesuit reached over and took the large piece for himself. The Franciscan indignantly said, "St. Francis always taught us to practice the virtue of temperance, taking only what we need." The Jesuit replied, "Then you should thank me for helping you to be so virtuous."

Catholics and Drinking

When it comes to the question of consuming alcohol, some Christians conclude that abstaining is the answer. Catholics, on the other hand, abide by the virtue of temperance. We can enjoy alcohol in moderation while regarding drunkenness as a sin. Jesus' first miracle was turning water into wine at the wedding feast at Cana (John 2:1–12) and he, along with his disciples, was accused of being a drunkard (Matthew 11:19) because they did not abstain from alcohol. In fact, the *Catholic Book of Blessings* includes a blessing of wine:

> Blessed are you, Lord God,
> who fill the hungry and satisfy the thirsty,
> and give us wine to gladden our hearts.
> Grant that all who drink this wine
> may rejoice in you
> and be invited to sit at your heavenly
> banquet
> for ever and ever.
> Amen.

The popular phrase "all things in moderation," which is a variation of Aristotle's rule of "moderation in all things," comes close to summarizing what the virtue of temperance is all about. However, temperance (combined with prudence) may lead us to decide that some things in life deserve to be avoided altogether!

Social Justice

In 2010, conservative talk-show host Glenn Beck encouraged listeners of his radio show to leave churches that preached social justice, claiming that the words "social justice" are code words for communism and Nazism. The backlash from many Christians, especially Catholics, was swift and strong. At the forefront of this response was Jesuit author and speaker Fr. James Martin, SJ, who explained in an article for *America* magazine that, to believe Beck would be to renounce an integral part of Catholic doctrine.

> The term "social justice" originated way back in the 1800s (and probably predates even that) and has been continually underlined by the Magisterium (the teaching authority of the church) and popes since Leo XIII, who began the modern tradition of Catholic social teaching with his encyclical on capital and labor, *Rerum Novarum* in 1891.

Martin went on to explain that, in 1971, the World Synod of Bishops in its document "Justice in the World," wrote that social justice was "a *constitutive* dimension of the Gospel." Martin quotes the late champion of social justice, Dom Helder Camara: "When I give food to the poor, they call me a saint. When I ask why the poor have no food, they call me a communist." In other words, while charity calls us to tend to the immediate needs of people, social justice calls us to ask the question, "What are the root causes of these needs?" Jesus' command to "love one another, even as I have loved you" (John 13:34) compels us to try to build a just society in which God's abundant love is manifested to all.

In particular, it is the responsibility of lay people to form our consciences according to the Gospel and Church teaching, and then, through our participation in the political process and our involvement in civic structures, to advocate for policies that respect the dignity of human beings and to seek to eliminate those policies that do not.

All of this to say that, when some people argue that religion has no place in politics, Catholics respond without doubt or hesitation that our faith cannot be separated from our responsibility to work for a more just society that respects the dignity of all human beings, from the moment of conception to the moment of natural death.

Practical suggestions for practicing the virtues and social justice:

> **Prudence**—stop and think before you act, discern what is best for all involved and the best course of action for achieving the good; avoid impulsive actions.

> **Justice**—consider the needs of others and always try to be fair; work for just conditions in your community and workplace.

> **Fortitude**—call on the strength to resist temptation; do what you know is right; be firm in the face of difficulty; resolve to overcome obstacles in your quest to lead a moral life; stand up for just causes even if it makes you unpopular.

> **Temperance**—moderate your desires for enjoyment and build self-control; seek balance in the use of created goods; model restraint in settings where others may engage in excess; practice modesty in the way you speak and dress.

> Contact your representatives in local and national government and urge them to take action on issues of social justice.

> Take seriously your responsibility to vote. Read and study the stances of candidates on social-justice issues and make informed decisions at the ballot box.

> Download the U.S. bishops' statement, *Forming Consciences for Faithful Citizenship* (from www.usccb.org) to learn more about political responsibility.

> Learn more about the Catholic Campaign for Human Development, the domestic antipoverty, social justice program of the U.S. Catholic bishops that seeks to address the root causes of poverty in America.

> Identify proactive groups in your community that are addressing issues of social justice and get involved in their efforts.

> Learn more about and support Catholic Relief Services, the official international humanitarian agency of the U.S. Catholic Church.

> Provide monetary support for community-based groups that are actively working to correct injustices in society.

> Learn more about issues of social justice: immigration, poverty, right to life, health care, employment, the environment, education, an end to the death penalty, human rights, fair trade, war and peace, and others and seek to get involved by sharing your time, talent, and treasure with efforts that address these issues.

Scripture

And if any one loves righteousness, her labors are virtues; for she teaches self-control and prudence, justice and courage; nothing in life is more profitable for mortals than these. (WISDOM 8:7)

Prayer

Good and gracious God, we often pray to you in the words that Jesus taught us, asking for the coming of your kingdom. Help us, Lord, to practice the virtues that reflect the values of your kingdom and help us work for justice, so that the world we live in may be transformed, showing the glory of your kingdom. Amen.

To share and learn more in a spiritual mentoring relationship about practicing the cardinal virtues and social justice, visit www.loyolapress.com/practice-makes-catholic.

Practice 12

Work for the Common Good

If charity is to be realistic and effective, it demands that The Gospel of Life be implemented also by means of certain forms of social activity and commitment in the political field, as a way of defending and promoting the value of life in our ever more complex and pluralistic societies. (*The Gospel of Life*, 88)

The Rules for Compassion

In an episode of *Seinfeld*, Jerry is sitting on one couch in his living room while his girlfriend is sitting on another couch, sobbing uncontrollably while watching the Bette Midler tearjerker *Beaches*. Jerry can't decide if the situation warrants a show of compassion. He thinks to himself, *Now what am I supposed to do here? Shall I go over there? It's not like somebody died. It's Beaches for god's sake. If she was sitting next to me I'd put my arm around her. I can't be making a big move like going all the way over there. I can't. I won't.* The next day, Jerry describes the situation to his friend George Costanza and the two of them together try to hash out the "rules" for showing compassion based on how close or how far away you're sitting from the person in need.

Needless to say, Jerry's rules are designed to guarantee the minimal amount of effort on his part.

On the other end of the spectrum are the Catholic Church's rules for showing compassion to others. Actually they aren't rules but principles or themes designed to help us answer the question posed in Luke 10:29, "Who is my neighbor?" Of course, the Catholic answer is a bit broader than Jerry's! In essence, we recognize that all people are our neighbors and we are called to care for them. The themes and principles that guide us to show compassion for our neighbors are collectively referred to as Catholic social teaching, which combines our commitment to community with our respect for the dignity of human life and commitment to social justice. Unlike Jerry's rules, which were designed to guarantee the least amount of effort on his part, Catholic social teaching stretches us to step out of our comfort zones and show compassion above and beyond the call of duty.

Catholic social teaching is organized around seven themes:

✚ **Life and Dignity of the Human Person**

✚ **Call to Family, Community, and Participation**

✚ **Rights and Responsibilities**

✚ **Option for the Poor and Vulnerable**

✚ **The Dignity of Work and the Rights of Workers**

✚ **Solidarity**

✚ **Care for God's Creation**

The Themes of Catholic Social Teaching

In the story of the Good Samaritan (Luke 10: 29–37) Jesus makes clear our responsibility to recognize those in need as our neighbors. The Church teaches this responsibility in the following themes of Catholic social teaching. Let's take a closer look at each.

"We're here to see if you practice what you preach."

✚ **Life and Dignity of the Human Person**—In the movie *Precious*, a sixteen-year-old African-American girl who is obese and illiterate is known by the name Precious. The painful irony of this story is that the girl is treated as anything *but* precious, suffering mental and physical abuse from both of her parents. Likewise, in the movie trilogy, *The Lord of the Rings*, the character Gollum refers to the ring that possesses magical powers, as "my precious."

By calling something *precious*, we attribute to it great value. We hold in great esteem what we label as precious. For Catholics, human life—beginning at the moment of conception—is considered precious. Our view of human life as sacred is the foundation of our moral vision. We recognize that many aspects of today's culture do not share this vision of human life. Excessive materialism and a lack of respect for the dignity of the human being threaten the foundation of a moral vision for society. Our belief in the life and dignity of the human person teaches us that all human life is sacred and that all people must be respected and valued over material goods. We are called to ask whether our actions as a society respect or threaten the life and dignity of the human person.

> We are called to ask whether our actions as a society respect or threaten the life and dignity of the human person.

➕ **Call to Family, Community, and Participation**—American heroes tend to be loners. From cowboys all the way up to contemporary heroes such as Batman and Ironman, one of the qualities most prevalent in American heroes is individualism, a trait that is close to the heart of many Americans. Although these heroes defend the vulnerable and are seen as the champions of justice, they are also quite clearly operating alone.

In general, American society worships the notion of individualism. In stark contrast to this, Catholic tradition preaches that human beings are not only sacred but also social. As such, we are called to support those principles and structures that foster community, beginning with the family, which is the building block of all communities. We believe that human beings grow and flourish best when participating in community life. Not only do we believe that it is an advantage to participate in community, but we also believe it is our duty, seeking to work together for the common good, especially for those who are poor and vulnerable.

Get Out the Vote!

In Chicago, known for more than its fair share of political shenanigans, there's a popular saying around election day: "Vote early and vote often!" Although the first part of the saying is laudable, the second part is not at all advisable! Truth be told, for Catholics, voting is considered not only a privilege but also a right and a responsibility. As part of our duty as citizens, the Church teaches us that it is "morally obligatory . . . to exercise the right to vote." (2240) The bishops of the United States teach us that "In the Catholic Tradition, responsible citizenship is a virtue, and participation in political life is a moral obligation." (*Faithful Citizenship*, 13) It would not be inconceivable for a Catholic to go to confession and utter the following words: "Bless me Father, for I have sinned; I failed to vote in the last election."

Cowboys are fun to watch, and their stories make for great entertainment. However, in baptism, the Church "lassos" us, corralling us away from individualism and making us members of a family, a community.

➕ **Rights and Responsibilities**—In the movie *Spiderman*, Peter Parker's Uncle Ben offers some sage advice: "Remember, with great power comes great responsibility." Uncle Ben is helping young Peter recognize that these are two sides of the same coin. Actually, this sounds a lot like what Jesus said in the Gospel of Luke: "From everyone to whom much has been given, much will be required; and from one to whom much has been entrusted, even more will be demanded" (Luke 12:48).

In today's society it is fashionable to talk about *rights*, especially when we feel that our own rights have been violated. We often fail, however, to focus on the other side of that coin, which is the concept of *responsibility*. As comedian Bill Maher (who, ironically, is stridently anti-religion) says, "We have a Bill of Rights. What we need is a Bill of Responsibilities." On this one topic, the Catholic Church agrees with him! While the Church teaches that every person has a right to life as well as a right to those things required for human decency, we also believe that it is our responsibility to protect these basic human rights—our own and the rights of others—in order to achieve a healthy society. We work to achieve a balance between protecting our rights and meeting our responsibilities to society. Because we have been given so much, we have a duty to one another, to our families, and to society as a whole.

➕ **Option for the Poor and Vulnerable**—One segment of our human community is especially vulnerable to misfortune, namely, those who are poor. Although many portions of our world enjoy the greatest prosperity known in human history, too many people continue to live in dire poverty.

Catholic social teaching reminds us that the best moral test for any society is to assess how our most vulnerable members are faring. Our tradition calls us to make a priority the needs of those who are poor and vulnerable. Jesus takes this even further, saying that how we treat those who are poor and vulnerable will be the main criteria by which we are judged (Matthew 25:31–46). We are called to pay special attention to the needs of the poor by defending and promoting their dignity and by meeting their immediate material needs.

➕ **The Dignity of Work and the Rights of Workers**—Poor Bob Cratchit! He worked under very poor conditions: the hours were too long, the pay was poor, his boss was a jerk, and to top it all off, his office was cold! Old man Scrooge wouldn't even let him toss a few extra pieces of coal into the furnace to take the chill out of the air.

A man visited the rectory and asked to see the pastor, who was well known for his charitable impulses. "Father," he said in a broken voice, "I wish to draw your attention to the terrible plight of a poor family in your parish. The mother is dead, the father has gambling debts and the nine children are starving. They are about to be put out on the streets with only the shirts on their backs because the father has only enough money to pay either the rent or his gambling debt but not both." "How terrible!" exclaimed the pastor. "May I ask who you are?" The sympathetic visitor dabbed his eyes with a handkerchief and sobbed, "I'm his bookie."

Charles Dickens' portrayal of the plight of workers in *A Christmas Carol* and in other novels such as *Oliver Twist* and *David Copperfield*, helped raise awareness of the terrible working conditions that workers, including children, faced in the nineteenth century.

Although we have come a long way in improving working conditions, many workers continue to labor under unfavorable conditions. The Catholic Church teaches that the basic rights of workers must be respected: the right to productive work, fair wages, and private property, and the right to organize, join unions, and pursue economic opportunity. Catholics believe that the economy is meant to serve people and that work is not merely a way to make a living but is an important way in which we participate in God's creation. By respecting and defending the rights of workers, we can protect human life, defend the rights of those who are vulnerable, honor the dignity of each individual, and advance the well-being of all people.

✚ **Solidarity**—Just before 33 Chilean miners were rescued after 2 months of being trapped deep underground in October, 2010, an amazing thing happened. Before even one miner was lifted up to safety, a rescuer descended into the depths of the mine. There he stood, in solidarity with the miners, symbolically sharing in their experience before seeing to it that they were lifted to safety one by one.

Solidarity is precisely this: standing with others during their time of trial. In a culture that is rampant with individualism, we are often tempted to turn inward and focus solely on our own needs. We can easily become indifferent to the needs of others and practice our own form of personal isolationism. However, Catholic social teaching reminds us that, because God is our Father, we are all brothers and sisters with the responsibility to care for one another. Through the incarnation of his Son Jesus, God saw fit to stand in solidarity with humanity, dwelling among us. As followers of Christ, we are called to stand in solidarity with others. Solidarity is the attitude that leads Christians to share spiritual and material goods. Solidarity

> "**From the depths of need and despair, people can work together, can organize themselves to solve their own problems and fill their own needs with dignity and strength.**"
> CESAR CHAVEZ

unites rich and poor, weak and strong, and helps create a society that recognizes our interdependence. In today's global village, we rely on solidarity to remind us that love of neighbor has global dimensions.

➕ **Care for God's Creation**—In 2010, the Gulf region of the United States experienced the worst ecological disaster in U.S. history when the Deepwater Horizon drilling rig exploded, resulting in over 50,000 barrels of crude oil gushing forth each day for months. All we could do was sit by and sadly watch as beautiful creatures such as pelicans and dolphins muddled through the murky goo, clinging to life.

> ## The Holy Childhood Association
>
> Since 1843, Catholic children have been taught to practice solidarity by participating in the Holy Childhood Association. The HCA, founded by French Bishop Charles de Forbin-Janson, invites Catholic children all over the world to learn about the needs of children who are poor, to pray for them, and to offer them financial help. In a 2003 message to the Holy Childhood Association, Pope John Paul II said that the HCA, "offers children in all dioceses of the world, a program that consists of prayer, sacrifice, and concrete acts of solidarity." Kids can learn how to practice solidarity through the Holy Childhood Association at www.hcakids.org.

Today more than ever, we are increasingly aware of the fragility of creation and of our responsibility for reducing our carbon footprints. The responsibility to care for all God has made is a requirement of our faith as well. Catholic social teaching reminds us that God is the creator of all people and all things and he wants us to enjoy his creation responsibly. To show respect for creation is to show respect for our Creator.

Catholicism's Best-Kept Secret

It has been said that the Catholic Church's social doctrine—including the themes of Catholic social teaching—is Catholicism's best-kept secret. Many people, including Catholics, are not aware of the Church's rich and powerful teachings on social issues and on the many ways we can influence society through the practice of our faith. It's time we Catholics let the cat out of the bag!

Practical suggestions for practicing the Catholic Social Teachings:

> **Life and Dignity of the Human Person**–show respect for people and demonstrate that you value all people over material goods; read and study the Church's teachings on life issues including abortion, embryonic stem-cell research, cloning, euthanasia, and the death penalty; visit the elderly; volunteer to help pregnant women in need; avoid talk that disrespects others, especially conversations that are prejudicial.

> **Call to Family, Community, and Participation**–support family life; work to build a community spirit in your neighborhood and workplace; work to promote the well-being of all, especially the poor and vulnerable; stay in contact with relatives, especially those who are aging; volunteer in your community; pray as a family; set aside time to spend with your family in recreation; participate in the political process.

> **Rights and Responsibilities**–Support causes that treat every human person as having a right to life and to those things required for human decency; practice stewardship (the responsibility of sharing time, talent, and treasure); educate yourself on the positions of various candidates and political parties on all issues and exercise your right and responsibility to vote in every election; work to ensure a quality education for all.

> **Option for the Poor and Vulnerable**–support efforts and agencies that promote and support the dignity of those in need; volunteer at a homeless shelter, food pantry, or soup kitchen; if you are an employer, pay a living wage and provide benefits that allow your employees to acquire what they need for a decent living.

> **The Dignity of Work and the Rights of Workers**–support efforts that challenge society to respect the basic rights of workers including the right to productive work, fair wages, and private property, and the right to organize, join unions, and pursue economic opportunity; affirm someone for a job well done; show appreciation and respect for all occupations; support local and independently owned businesses; share your job skills with others; support fair trade.

> **Solidarity**–recognize that we are all brothers and sisters with the responsibility to care for one another; share both spiritual and material goods; work to create a society that recognizes that we all depend on one another; promote and participate in ecumenical and inter-faith dialogue and activities; participate in parish-sharing programs and diocesan partnership programs (i.e. parishes/dioceses partner with parishes/dioceses in other parts of the world); learn more about people of other ethnic backgrounds, religions, and cultures; support student-exchange programs.

> **Care for God's Creation**–Enjoy God's creation and accept the responsibility to care for it; support growers of organically grown foods; plant a garden; avoid products that harm the environment; walk or bike instead of driving a car when possible; support neighborhood cleanup projects; reduce you carbon footprint; recycle.

Scripture

"Which of these three, do you think, was a neighbor to the man who fell into the hands of the robbers?" He said, "The one who showed him mercy." Jesus said to him, "Go and do likewise." (LUKE 10:36–37)

Prayer

Lord God, you sent your only Son, Jesus, to bring glad tidings to the poor, recovery of sight to the blind, and freedom for captives. Help me participate in your mission by living the principles of Catholic social teaching. Open my eyes to recognize all people as my neighbors and all of creation as your gift to be nurtured and cared for. Amen.

To share and learn more in a spiritual mentoring relationship about practicing the Catholic social teachings, visit www.loyolapress.com/practice-makes-catholic.

Practice 13

Keep the Ten Commandments

The Lord prescribed love towards God and taught justice towards neighbor, so that man would be neither unjust, nor unworthy of God. Thus, through the Decalogue, God prepared man to become his friend and to live in harmony with his neighbor. . . . The words of the Decalogue remain likewise for us Christians. Far from being abolished, they have received amplification and development from the fact of the coming of the Lord in the flesh. (St. Irenaeus, Adv. haeres., 4,16, 3-4: PG 7/1,1017-1018)

The Rules

My wife and I have been happily married since 1982—you can do the math. Over the course of so many years, spouses develop certain little rules to abide by. For example, I am forbidden to tickle the bottom of my wife's feet. Apparently they are so sensitive that she just can't stand to be tickled there. I am also forbidden to call her Jo Jo (her name is Joanne). Of course, if I really want to annoy her, I would tickle her feet while calling her Jo Jo!

Relationships have rules. When we want a relationship to work, we establish rules to protect ourselves, one another, and the relationship. The rules I mentioned above are silly examples—real, but silly. In reality, my wife and I have established many rules over the years—some spoken and many unspoken—that serve to maintain our relationship and enable us to show how much we love each other. These rules ensure that we treat each other with respect, show concern and compassion, and work at being thoughtful and unselfish. Each time we do something that hurts the other, a new rule is established or an old one is reinforced. Rules are needed if love is to thrive.

Our relationship with God is governed by rules as well. Not because God is a taskmaster who delights in making people follow rules, but because God's chosen people—our ancestors in faith, the Israelites—desired to preserve this new and wonderful relationship with God that had blossomed as a result of the Exodus experience. Eager to stay in God's good graces, the people told Moses, "Go near, you yourself, and hear all that the LORD our God will say. Then tell us everything that the LORD our God tells you, and we will listen and do it." (Deuteronomy 5:27) This is the biblical equivalent of a teenager telling his or her newfound love, "I'll do anything just to be with you."

> **Rules are needed if love is to thrive.**

Imagine their joy when Moses returned from the mountaintop with only ten rules that they needed to follow in order to enjoy a loving relationship with the Creator of the universe! In fact, they did indeed rejoice when Moses gave them the Ten Commandments: "Everything that the LORD has spoken, we will do" (Exodus 19:8), which, of course, is the biblical equivalent of that same infatuated teenager saying "I'll never leave you."

In some cases, infatuation dies out once the parties involved realize that there really *are* things they will have to do if they want to stay in their lover's good graces. In other cases, that same realization allows the relationship to grow from infatuation to love. Whatever the case, love grows when people abide by the rules established to protect the relationship.

> **"It is not that we keep His commandments first, and that then He loves; but that He loves us, and then we keep His commandments."**
> ST. AUGUSTINE

Too often, we tend to think of the Ten Commandments as rules that solely prohibit us from doing certain things. We think of them as rules that say no. In reality, the commandments are rules that enable us to say yes to our relationship with God and with one another. Any time we say yes to someone or something, we have to say no to other things.

Love of God

The first three commandments help us say yes to God and to show our love for him. The remaining seven commandments show us how to say yes to a loving relationship with

> **The first three Commandments help us say yes to God and to show our love for him.**

our neighbors. Love of God is summarized as worshipping God alone, honoring God's name, and keeping holy the Lord's Day.

 THE FIRST COMMANDMENT *I am the Lord your God. You shall have no other gods before me.*

Every building needs a firm foundation. The first commandment provides a strong foundation for the other nine and for our lives. False gods are anything that we look to for ultimate fulfillment instead of seeking that fulfillment from God. To practice the first commandment is to enjoy what life offers while recognizing that God alone ultimately sustains and fulfills us.

 THE SECOND COMMANDMENT *You shall not take the name of the Lord your God in vain.*

Brand names stand for something. Toyota has long stood for quality, innovation, and reliability in cars. A wave of recalls in 2009 and 2010, however, did much to tarnish the Toyota name. God's name stands for something as well. When we practice the second commandment we not only refrain from cursing with God's name but we also honor what God's name stands for: love, forgiveness, justice, peace, mercy, compassion, and so on.

 THE THIRD COMMANDMENT *Keep holy the Sabbath day.*

In the movie *Apollo 13*, a dramatic scene shows the space crew making a course correction using their damaged ship without the assistance of an onboard computer. In order to complete the maneuver successfully, astronaut James Lovell (played by Tom Hanks) explains that as long as they

" 'God is love' . . . a verse apparently out of fashion the year they designed our sanctuary."

keep focused on one fixed point in space—Earth—they'll be able to complete the burn successfully. For a tense thirty seconds, the crew flies the ship manually, keeping Earth fixed in their window as they complete the burn, successfully putting them back on course for a safe reentry. For us, every Sunday is a course correction. To live the third commandment is to take this one day a week—Sunday—to refocus our attention on God as our "fixed point" so that we can be guided home safely.

I Learned That in Kindergarten!

When Cardinal Joseph Ratzinger became Pope Benedict XVI, many people speculated on what his first encyclical would be about and what his writing style would be. After all, he is considered to be a highly intellectual, complex, and brilliant theologian. Would he be able to write something that the average Catholic could even understand? To the surprise of many, Benedict offered *Deus Caritas Est*, which means "God is love," as his first encyclical in 2005. This complex theologian chose to share a message of great simplicity that we all learned when we were in kindergarten: God is love. The message of this encyclical is simple but not simplistic: love is more than a feeling, and love of God and love of neighbor *cannot* be separated.

Love of Neighbor

Love of neighbor cannot be separated from love of God, and vice versa. The Catholic way recognizes that God *is* love and that when we abide in love (live in loving relationships), we abide in God. We show love of neighbor not to please God but as a way of encountering God. Love of neighbor is not simply the avoidance of doing anything to harm a neighbor but is the active effort to ensure that all our neighbors are treated fairly and justly and have everything they need for human decency.

> **Love of neighbor cannot be separated from love of God and vice versa.**

Love of neighbor is summarized as honoring our parents and those in authority, respecting all human life, having a reverence for sexuality, respecting the possessions of others, living in the truth, and avoiding excessive desire for that which belongs to others.

✚ THE FOURTH COMMANDMENT *Honor your father and your mother*

When children play the game "Simon Says," they learn how to listen to a voice of authority. The message is clear: if you don't follow the voice of authority correctly, you're OUT! God is the author of all life. He shares his authority with certain people who are called to lead others to follow him. Parents, in particular, are delegated by God to represent his authority in the home. By extension, teachers, coaches, catechists, and others share this authority by representing the parents in various situations. Finally, legitimately elected/appointed government leaders also share in God's authority as they work for the common good. To live the fourth commandment is to honor God's authority by honoring those who legitimately represent that authority in our everyday lives.

✚ THE FIFTH COMMANDMENT *You shall not kill.*

Once, when my wife and I vacationed in Marco Island, Florida, it happened to be turtle nesting season. Signs everywhere warned us about the need to protect these fragile animals. With all respect to turtles and other wildlife, the fact remains that human life holds a special place in the eyes of God. To practice the fifth commandment is not only to refrain from homicide, which most of us do quite readily, but is also to monitor all of our actions, ensuring that we are protecting the fragility, dignity,

Anger and the Fifth Commandment

More and more on the news, we hear about people being angry. Voters are angry with incumbents. Employees are angry with employers. Liberals are angry with conservatives and conservatives are angry with liberals. The fact is, anger can be righteous when its overriding goal is to correct an injustice and bring people back into right relationship with one another. Too often, however, anger degenerates into a desire for revenge. In and of itself, anger is a normal human emotion that we need to channel and control. However, when anger reaches the point of wishing another person harm or expressing hatred toward him or her, it is a violation of the fifth commandment. Instead, we are called to work for peace, which is not to be equated with passivity. We make a conscious effort to build harmony among people.

and sacredness of all human life—from the moment of conception to the moment of natural death—and are avoiding any actions that might cause harm, physically and otherwise, to any of our neighbors.

➕ **THE SIXTH COMMANDMENT** *You shall not commit adultery.*

When you go to the doctor for a routine physical, he or she will test your reflexes by asking you to cross your legs and then tapping you with a small hammer-like object just below the knee. If you're healthy, your leg will instantly kick forward. A reflex is an involuntary response to a stimulus. As sexual beings, we are wired to respond physically to sexual stimuli. This doesn't mean, however, that we have no control over this response. To practice the sixth commandment is to properly control and channel our sexual desires in order to respect relationships.

➕ **THE SEVENTH COMMANDMENT** *You shall not steal.*

When our son Mike was a little guy, we took him to a local grocery store to participate in an Easter egg hunt. When they blew the whistle to start, my wife and I were never more afraid for our son's safety! Parents recklessly whisked their kids up and down the store aisles, greedily grabbing for every Easter egg they could get their hands on lest their child

A middle-aged man was upset because he had lost his favorite hat. He was too cheap to buy a new one so he decided to go to church and steal one from the coat room while the ushers were busy taking up the collection. It just so happened that the pastor was preaching on the Ten Commandments that day and, after listening to the homily, the man changed his mind about stealing a hat. After Mass, the man met the pastor at the door and said, "Thanks, Father, for saving my soul today. I came to church today to steal a hat but after hearing you preach about the Ten Commandments, I decided against it. The priest answered, "Ah, so what I said about the 7th Commandment—You shall not steal—helped you have a change of heart?" "No," responded the man, "when you started talking about the 6th Commandment—You shall not commit adultery—I suddenly remembered where I left my hat."

come up with fewer than the others. We quickly gathered up our son, left the store, and vowed "never again!" Unfortunately, many of us continue to operate in life with the same flawed assumption that there's not enough to go around so we need to hoard whatever we can get our hands on. In practicing the seventh commandment, we certainly avoid theft. But we also learn to be satisfied with what we have, recognizing that God provides abundantly for his people as long as we learn to share properly.

➕ **THE EIGHTH COMMANDMENT** *You shall not bear false witness against your neighbor.*

Watch people's body language when they're bowling to see what they do when the ball they've just thrown veers a bit off center. They step to the side and tilt their head to make the shot appear to be straight on target. Batters do the same thing in baseball when they hit a long fly that starts to veer foul. It's as if we think we can alter reality by looking at it differently. Unfortunately, we sometimes do this in life. When something we do or say veers off course, instead of looking at it truthfully, we sometimes try to look at it from another angle, hoping that will make it all right. To practice the eighth commandment is to see and speak of things as they truly are instead of creating an alternate "reality" that is nothing more than falsehood.

✚ THE NINTH COMMANDMENT *You shall not covet your neighbor's wife*

It's common nowadays for many homes to be equipped with water filters for drinking water. Many of us are rightly concerned that the water coming into our homes may not be as pure as we think. Water filters remove the impurities, enabling us to enjoy fresh, pure water. Sometimes, our minds and hearts can become polluted with desires that are not pure. To practice the ninth commandment is to allow our impure desires, especially those desires for people who are already living in commitment to someone else, to be purified by the grace of God and to instead recognize that our deepest desire is to be one with God.

✚ THE TENTH COMMANDMENT *You shall not covet your neighbor's goods*

There's a saying that "the grass is always greener on the other side of the fence." We often think that what others have is better than what we have. To practice the tenth commandment is to recognize the good things we have and to be thankful for them so that we do not covet or desire the belongings of others. This commandment teaches us not to compare ourselves with others but to appreciate what we have.

A Plan for Living

God has equipped his people with a basic plan for living. Part of that plan is outlined in the Ten Commandments. Although we tend to think of the Commandments as prohibitions that strictly tell us what not to do, in reality, the Commandments are meant to guide us to make choices that allow us to live as God wants us to live: in close relationship with him and with one another.

Practical suggestions for practicing the commandments:

> **First Commandment:** Identify what you tend to be preoccupied with and where (how) you are seeking fulfillment other than from God.

> **Second Commandment:** Begin each day with the Sign of the Cross as a reminder that you are about to do all things in God's name. Remind yourself throughout the day that your words and actions are to honor God's good name.

Examination of Conscience

A common practice of Catholics is to do an examination of conscience; it's a way of calling to mind our sins, especially before going to confession. One of the most popular ways of examining conscience is to use the Ten Commandments as the basis for such a review. Here's how to do an examination of conscience:

> Set aside some quiet time for prayerful reflection, perhaps fifteen to twenty minutes.

> Begin by asking the Holy Spirit to guide you in your examination and to help you be honest with yourself.

> Read through a set of questions based on the Ten Commandments (examples can be found in Catholic prayer books and online such as http://www.loyolapress.com/an-examination-of-conscience.htm) and honestly reflect on your thoughts and actions associated with each one.

> You may consider journaling about these reflections.

> Identify those areas where you most need forgiveness and, especially in the case of serious sin, confess these to a priest in the sacrament of penance and reconciliation.

> **Third Commandment:** Review how you spend your Sundays and ask yourself what you could do to make the day more of an opportunity to refocus on your relationship with God.

> **Fourth Commandment:** Consider your attitude toward those in authority, beginning with your family life, and identify ways that you can honor those in authority.

> **Fifth Commandment:** Review moments of anger and feelings of hatred that you've experienced recently and strive to identify the underlying causes. Pray for the well-being of those to whom you've directed those feelings of anger and/or hatred. Work for the protection of the unborn and for all those who are vulnerable.

> **Sixth Commandment:** Avoid any form of entertainment that distorts the meaning of sexuality.

> **Seventh Commandment:** Give an honest day's work for your salary and consider the needs of those who have less than you.

- **Eighth Commandment:** Refrain from gossip and allow others the benefit of the doubt before jumping to conclusions.
- **Ninth and Tenth Commandments:** Be happy for the prosperity of others and avoid envy of their possessions or their relationships.
- Practice an examination of conscience on a regular basis, especially before celebrating the sacrament of penance and reconciliation.
- Take advantage of opportunities to celebrate the sacrament of penance and reconciliation as a way to strengthen your resolve to keep the Ten Commandments.

Scripture

"Teacher, which commandment in the law is the greatest?' He said to him, ' "You shall love the Lord your God with all your heart, and with all your soul, and with all your mind." This is the greatest and first commandment. And a second is like it: "You shall love your neighbor as yourself." On these two commandments hang all the law and the prophets." (MATTHEW 22:36–40)

Prayer

Good and gracious God, when your people Israel sought to remain in close relationship with you, you provided the Ten Commandments, showing them how to love you and one another. Help me recognize that I cannot separate my love for you from my love for neighbor. Help me say yes to you by saying no to anything that interferes with our relationship. Amen.

To share and learn more in a spiritual mentoring relationship about practicing the Ten Commandments, visit www.loyolapress.com/practice-makes-catholic.

PART FOUR

A REVERENCE FOR SCRIPTURE AND TRADITION

For a journalist, a reliable source can be a person, another publication, or perhaps some document or record. When journalists report, listeners or readers want to know the source of the information and whether or not those sources are reliable.

When it comes to religion, it helps to know the source of the information we are being asked to embrace as the truth. For Protestants, that source is Scripture and Scripture alone. For Catholics, we identify our source as Scripture and Tradition—not two sources, but one single source that comes to us in two ways. Scripture, of course, is the written Word of God's self-revelation. "Tradition" refers to the Church's efforts over the course of two thousand-plus years to interpret and apply the word of God to the experience of each generation. The result is a rich heritage of teaching, grounded in Scripture, that comes to us through the lives and writings of the saints and the teachings of the Church as handed down through Church documents and writings. In this part of the book, we'll look at the following Catholic practices related to our reverence for Scripture and Tradition:

Practice 14: Make a Pilgrimage

Practice 15: Befriend the Saints

Practice 16: Study Scripture, Tradition, and Catholic Literature

Practice 17: Learn Traditional Prayers

To share and learn more in a spiritual mentoring relationship about practicing the Catholic reverence for Scripture and Tradition, visit www.loyolapress.com/practice-makes-catholic.

Practice 14

Make a Pilgrimage

Pilgrimages, a sign of the condition of the disciples of Christ in this world, have always held an important place in the life of Christians. In the course of history, Christians have always walked to celebrate their faith in places that indicate a memory of the Lord or in sites representing important moments in the history of the Church. For the Church, pilgrimages, in all their multiple aspects, have always been a gift of grace. (*The Pilgrimage in the Great Jubilee Year*, John Paul II, 1998)

Are We There Yet?

There are two kinds of vacations. In the first kind, we fly to our destination, tolerating airports and airplanes, so that we can arrive as quickly as possible and begin enjoying ourselves. In the second kind, we drive to our destination, stopping along the way and enjoying the ride. In the second kind, the traveling itself is part of the vacation experience. It is a journey with adventures along the way. This second kind of vacation is a metaphor for life: we are on a journey with a destination in mind, but the journey itself is part of the experience.

We are indeed on a journey to life with God in the fullness of his kingdom. However, our life on earth is not merely something to be tolerated as we await our true destination. Rather, our life on earth is a journey, and we encounter God along the way. As Catholics, we symbolize this journey by making pilgrimages to holy places.

A pilgrimage is not merely a trip to a destination. The traveling itself is an experience that symbolizes life's journey, often filled with hardships, but also with great joys and wonderful relationships. Participants in a pilgrimage are not just travelers—they are pilgrims. To be a pilgrim is to be on a sacred journey in search of fulfillment in God. As a Church, we are a "pilgrim people," traveling together toward our God. We do not simply endure this world, nor do we disdain this world and focus solely on the afterlife. In fact, in *Lumen Gentium*, the Pastoral Constitution on the Church in the Modern World, the bishops of the Second Vatican Council remind us that our destination sheds light on the meaning of our pilgrimage:

> Christians, on pilgrimage toward the heavenly city, should seek and think of these things which are above. This duty in no way decreases, rather it increases, the importance of their obligation to work with all men in the building of a more human world. Indeed, the mystery of the Christian faith furnishes them with an excellent stimulant and aid to fulfill this duty more courageously and especially to uncover the full meaning of this activity, one which gives to human culture its eminent place in the integral vocation of man. (57)

For Christians, pilgrimages began in the centuries following the death, resurrection, and ascension of Jesus Christ. As Christianity spread, pilgrims sought to visit the sites connected with important moments in the life of Jesus. References to Christian pilgrimages date back to the fourth century. Church Fathers such as Saint Augustine of Hippo and Saint Jerome wrote about and encouraged pilgrimages. As time went on and Christianity continued to spread, it became customary for people to make pilgrimages closer to home, visiting shrines and holy sites associated with the saints and martyrs and eventually, apparitions of the Blessed Virgin Mary.

At various points in life, Catholics make pilgrimages to sacred places: the Holy Land, the Vatican, birthplaces of saints, cathedrals, shrines,

As a Church, we are a "pilgrim people," traveling together toward God.

basilicas, and other holy sites to recommit ourselves to the great journey of life and to remind ourselves of our true destination—fullness of life with the Father, Son, and Holy Spirit. We do so to remind ourselves that we are not alone on this journey and that the journey itself is where we encounter God. We make pilgrimage to open our eyes to the presence of God on this earthly journey until that day when we shall see God face-to-face at our final destination.

A pilgrimage is not the same thing as a tour. A pilgrimage has a specific spiritual flavor to it; it is a spiritual quest to grow closer to God made manifest in a physical journey to a sacred space where we may encounter God in a special way. A Catholic pilgrimage forms community as pilgrims travel together, get to know one another, and pray for one another along the way. Formal Catholic pilgrimages are escorted by a spiritual leader, usually a priest, who facilitates prayer and spiritual exercises as well as the celebration of the sacraments along the way. Pilgrims don't seek to visit tourist attractions, but to grow in faith, to practice prayer, to seek healing, to find direction, to pray for others, to accompany a loved one on a spiritual quest, to seek forgiveness of and practice penance for sins, or to express thanks and praise.

Catholics think of a pilgrimage as a calling. Some people say that you do not select a pilgrimage destination but that the pilgrimage destination selects you. What the pilgrim senses is a longing or yearning. When we pay attention, we recognize our own spiritual journey and a physical journey that externalizes it. Pilgrims often pack less than tourists do because a big

> ## Most Popular Catholic Pilgrimage Destinations
>
> Among the most popular destinations for Catholic pilgrimages are the following:
>
> - > The Holy Land
> - > The Vatican
> - > Assisi, Italy
> - > Lourdes, France
> - > Basilica of Our Lady of Guadalupe, Mexico
> - > Fatima, Portugal
> - > Montserrat, Spain
> - > Santiago de Compostela, Galicia, Spain
> - > Constantinople (Istanbul), Turkey
> - > Knock, Ireland

> A priest was waiting in a long line at the airport, on his way to participating in a pilgrimage over the Christmas holidays. After what seemed like forever, he finally made it to the security check point where the security agent said, "Sorry about the delay, Father. It seems as if everyone waits until the last minute to get ready for a long trip." The priest chuckled, "I know what you mean. It's the same in my business."

part of the pilgrimage experience is placing trust in God by leaving behind many of the securities of everyday living. This embracing of poverty captures the spirit of G. K. Chesterton's famous words, "The rich choose their adventures. The poor have their adventures chosen for them."

As a pilgrimage begins, attention is given to the departure, since many pilgrims seek to leave behind some undesirable part of their lives. Along the way, pilgrims participate in spiritual disciplines designed to raise awareness of the presence and movement of God in their lives and on the journey and to detach from everyday concerns. Some examples of pilgrimage disciplines: fasting, walking long distances, participating in processions, reading spiritual literature, praying devotions, and performing acts of penance. Arriving at a destination is, of course, important, because the goal of the pilgrimage is to arrive in the presence of God, a place where we are transformed.

"They spent two hundred years building and three hundred years on the capital funds drive."

One of the most popular Catholic pilgrimages in recent years has been World Youth Day, a practice begun by Pope John Paul II in 1986. This weeklong international event is held every two or three years and draws hundreds of thousands of Catholic youth from all over the world to the host city. The young pilgrims who attend often exchange flags, T-shirts, sacramentals, and other souvenirs with their fellow pilgrims from other countries. Throughout the week, youth participate in catechetical sessions with bishops, have opportunities for the sacrament of reconciliation, attend Christian rock concerts, participate in prayer, and visit sacred sites in the host city. In addition to making the pilgrimage to the host country, the young pilgrims often participate in walks of many miles to the various events, especially the papal Mass, which is the climax of the event. In 1995, the World Youth Day in Manila, Philippines, attracted over five million young pilgrims!

> **"Life itself is a pilgrimage. Every day is different, every day can have a magic moment."**
> PAULO COELHO

Visiting Churches on Holy Thursday

Many Catholics participate in a local mini-pilgrimage on the evening of Holy Thursday, following the Mass of the Lord's Supper. This liturgy ends with a procession of the Blessed Sacrament, which is then placed in reposition (on a special altar) so that the faithful may remain in vigil until 11 p.m. or midnight. As a result, Catholic churches are unlocked on this evening, providing Catholics with an opportunity to visit a variety of parishes, especially in urban areas where a cluster of churches may be within just a few miles of one another. Traditionally, Catholics visit seven parishes on this night (symbolic of the ancient practice of visiting the seven basilicas of Rome as an act of penance), ideally ending up at the cathedral of the diocese. However, this mini-pilgrimage can take any shape or form depending on your circumstances. The goal is to spend a few minutes in each church, praying before the Blessed Sacrament, and keeping vigil on the night that Jesus prayed in the Garden of Gethsemane before his arrest, asking his disciples to stay awake with him.

Relics

Because Catholics are sacramental, we do not drive a wedge between spirit and matter. Thus, we encounter grace through physical things. One such example is relics—the bones, clothing, ashes, or possessions of the saints we hold in reverence. Many people undertake pilgrimages to visit sites where such relics are held. We don't believe relics have magical powers that we can use to compel God to work in a certain way. But we do believe that God uses the physical realities of this world to touch our lives. Just as Jesus' lifeless body was treated with reverence by Joseph of Arimathea, Nicodemus, Mary the mother of Jesus, and the women who came to the tomb following his death, we show reverence for the bodies of the saints. In the fourth century, St. Jerome described the Catholic understanding of relics: "We do not worship, we do not adore, for fear that we should bow down to the creature rather than to the creator, but we venerate the relics of the martyrs in order the better to adore him whose martyrs they are" (*Ad Riparium*, i, P.L., XXII, 907).

Practical suggestions for practicing pilgrimages:

> Visit the Catholic parishes in your area. Learn about their history and architecture.

> Walk to church instead of driving as a reminder of the spiritual journey on which you are a participant.

> Make arrangements to celebrate the Eucharist at your diocese's cathedral. Visit your diocesan website for background information on the history of the diocese, the cathedral, and the bishops.

> Visit a local monastery and learn about the monastic way of life that has been part of Church life for more than fifteen hundred years.

> Identify locations of shrines and basilicas in your area and make arrangements to visit them.

> On vacations, stop at various cathedrals and shrines along the way. For a list of shrines in the United States, visit www.catholicshrines.net.

> Consider participating, at least once in your lifetime, in a full-fledged pilgrimage to a holy site such as the Holy Land, the Vatican, Fatima,

Lourdes, Assisi, Manresa (St. Ignatius of Loyola), or Mexico City (Our Lady of Guadalupe).

> On Holy Thursday, participate in a mini-pilgrimage, visiting churches in your area after the evening Mass of the Lord's Supper.

> Remind yourself each day that you are a pilgrim on a journey, with God as your starting point *and* your destination.

> Establish sacred sites of your own: locations in your life where you have had an experience of God's presence. This can include visiting cemeteries where our belief in the communion of saints is expressed in a tangible manner. Visit these sites often.

Scripture

Now every year his parents went to Jerusalem for the festival of the Passover. And when he was twelve years old, they went up as usual for the festival. (Luke 2:41–42)

Prayer

Loving God, you called Abram and Sarai to set out on a journey of faith. You led your people Israel on a journey of faith through the desert for forty years. You call me to embark on a journey of faith with your son Jesus, guided by the Holy Spirit. Help me recognize this life as an earthly pilgrimage, keeping my eyes open for signs of your presence, and savoring the moments of grace that surround me, until that day when I arrive at my destination, in your divine presence. Amen.

To share and learn more in a spiritual mentoring relationship about practicing pilgrimage, visit www.loyolapress.com/practice-makes-catholic.

Practice 14: Make a Pilgrimage

Practice 15

Befriend the Saints

When we read the lives of the saints, their teachings and witness, we can be motivated to holiness by their example which was shaped by the Holy Spirit. (*United States Catholic Catechism for Adults*, p. 106)

Getting to Know You

Do you remember a time when you wanted to know someone better? How did you go about developing that relationship? Most likely, you spent time together getting to know more about each other. One of the ways that we get to know someone is by knowing *about* him or her. "Where do you work? What do you do for a living? Where are you from? What are your hobbies?" Over time, we develop a clearer image of the person.

In a similar way, one of the ways that we deepen our relationship with Jesus and come to know him more intimately is by knowing about him. In Catholic tradition, we call this *study*. Like a teenager who is filled with infatuation and cannot take his or her eyes off the person who has become the object of desire, we cannot take our minds off Jesus. Unlike the passing teenage infatuation, however, our desire becomes a lifelong endeavor to know Jesus more intimately and to become more like him.

Monkey See, Monkey Do

None of us is purely original. The fact is, we human beings learn by imitation. As infants, we begin making sounds that imitate the sounds made by those around us. Before long, we are shaping words with those sounds, achieving the ability to communicate with others. Our imitation doesn't stop there, however. Scientists have shown that imitation cannot be dismissed as some sort of lower form of learning but is a quite sophisticated intellectual activity. Simply defined, imitation is when one individual observes the actions and behaviors of another and then replicates them. What's interesting, though, is that this kind of imitation does not lead to conformity, because each of us must work at adapting the behaviors we see to our unique abilities and circumstances. And so imitating the actions and behaviors of others can actually help us become the unique persons God calls us to be. For this reason, Catholics do not hesitate to look to the saints as people worthy of imitating.

One of the ways that we get to know someone is by knowing *about* them.

For Catholics, study takes on many shapes and forms: reading Catholic literature, visiting Catholic Web sites, attending faith formation sessions, to name a few. One of the most tried and true forms of Catholic study is

In an attempt to live holy lives, two friends decided to read *The Lives of the Saints*. Concluding that most of the saints achieved major accomplishments in the name of the Gospel, they decided to make an important statement about caring for the environment by protesting pollution caused by oil rigs. One of the men bravely stepped into the Gulf of Mexico and started walking toward an offshore oil rig. The other was caught by surprise but quickly followed in pursuit. As the first man continued on his way with the water only coming up to his ankles, the other man began to panic for the water was now up to his neck. He called out to the first man, "Go on without me! You're obviously more saintly than I since you can walk on water as our Lord did!" to which his friend replied, "You dummy, walk on the pipeline like I am!"

learning about the lives of the saints. By learning about the saints and how their relationships with the risen Christ transformed their lives, we seek to grow closer to Christ and experience transformation for ourselves. Because human beings learn through imitation, it should come as no surprise that as we seek to grow spiritually, we look to other people—parents, godparents, and others who, by example, show us how to follow Jesus. By imitating the saints even in small ways, we can learn how to respond to God's call in our own lives. In his book *My Life with the Saints* (Loyola Press), Fr. Jim Martin, SJ explains how this happens:

Imitating the actions and behaviors of others can actually help us become the unique persons God is calling us to be.

> There's no reason to feel as if devotion to the saints somehow takes away from your devotion to Jesus: everything the saints say and do is centered on Christ and points us in his direction. In reading the lives of the saints, I also discovered that I could easily recognize myself, or at least parts of myself, in their stories. This was the aspect of their lives that I most appreciated: they had struggled with the same human foibles that everyone does. Knowing this, in turn, encouraged me to pray to them for help during particular times and for particular needs. (p. 7)

Studying the lives of the saints is not a form of living in the past. Historians study the past, but that doesn't mean they must conform to the culture they are studying. Catholics, on the other hand, have a profound sense of continuity because of our understanding of Tradition; we see the past, present, and future as

IMAGINE IF WE HAD THIS KIND OF SEATING CAPACITY IN THE CATACOMBS!

The early Christians' enthusiasm was contagious.

a whole. While we recognize that the Church is part of history, we also believe that the Church transcends history. The men and women we call saints have transcended history and have entered our lives of faith, providing ongoing inspiration for each succeeding generation. One of the most beneficial aspects of studying the saints is our discovery that holiness comes in many shapes and sizes. Some saints were quiet while others were loud. Some were intellectuals while others were uneducated. Some wrote volumes while others did not record a single word. Some were known for wise sayings while others were known only by their actions.

> It is no stretch to say that the saints take center stage in Catholic life.

Our emphasis on the connection of the saints of the past with the experience of the present and our hope for the future is most evident in our celebration of the liturgy. At various times throughout the Mass and especially in the eucharistic prayer, we invoke the intercession of the saints to

Even the Saints Imitated the Saints

One of the most famous saints is St. Ignatius of Loyola. What's interesting about his story is that his conversion was hastened by his own study of the Christian saints who had gone before him. Ignatius was born in 1491 into a large family of nobility in Spain. In his youth and young adulthood, Ignatius dreamed of knighthood and of accomplishing great military victories. However, in 1521 Ignatius was seriously wounded in a battle with the French, taking a cannon ball to the leg. While Ignatius was recuperating, the only reading materials he had to occupy his time were stories of the lives of Jesus and the saints. Reading about these great people who sought to follow Jesus inspired Ignatius to turn his life over to the Lord and to live a life that would bring honor and glory to God's name. Ignatius went on to found the religious community known as the Jesuits (the Society of Jesus) and became an expert in the area of spirituality, writing his *Spiritual Exercises*, which continue to guide people to find God in all things. Today, many people seek to imitate Ignatius who himself imitated saints in his quest to imitate Christ.

help us grow closer to God and to do God's will. Likewise, the liturgical calendar, as pointed out in Practice 2, sets aside many dates throughout the year to honor individual saints. Because the liturgy is the "source and summit" of the Christian life (*Catechism of the Catholic Church* #1324) and the saints have such a place of prominence in our celebration of the liturgy, it is no stretch to say that the saints take center stage in Catholic life.

> **"Every saint has a past and every sinner has a future."**
> OSCAR WILDE

Unfortunately, for Christianity as a whole, devotion to the saints took a hit at the time of the Protestant Reformation which sought to reform some abuses surrounding the practice. As a result, many of our Protestant brothers and sisters look with suspicion on our devotion to the saints, questioning the need for their intercession. Within Catholicism, however, studying the lives of the saints has enabled many Catholics, especially those for whom the study of theology was out of reach, to deepen their faith. More important, the saints provided and continue to provide us with real-life examples of how the Gospel can and should be lived. In a sense, their lives provide us with a pattern so that we, too, can follow Christ more closely and lead lives of holiness. Even though many of these saints lived centuries ago, their lives continue to be relevant to our current situations.

Fortunately for us, many saints recorded their thoughts and feelings in great works of literature, history, and inspiration. Saints such as Augustine, Thomas Aquinas, Teresa of Ávila, Ignatius, and Catherine of Siena, have left behind profound writings that take us deep into their hearts, minds, and souls. Not only are we able to read about them, but in many cases, we are able to hear them speak directly to us about their relationship with God.

Practical suggestions for practicing study of the lives of the saints:

> Visit reliable Catholic Web sites dedicated to the lives of the saints (for example, www.catholic.org/saints or www.americancatholic.org/features/saints).

The Butler Did It

When it comes to reading the lives of the saints, one of the most prominent resources is *Butler's Lives of the Saints*. Alban Butler was a Roman Catholic priest in England in the eighteenth century who studied the saints for more than thirty years and collected his hagiography (a study of the saints) into four volumes (over 2500 saints) that were published in 1756-59. Since then, Butler's work has gone through many translations and editions. Today there are multiple resources—in printed or electronic form—from which to learn about these heroes and heroines of our Catholic story.

> Read and study books about the lives of the saints such as *Butler's Lives of the Saints* (Concise, Modernized Edition, Paraclete Press) or *My Life with the Saints* (Loyola Press). Contact a local Catholic bookstore for recommendations.

> Read books about specific saints such as Teresa of Avila, Ignatius of Loyola, Francis of Assisi, Paul the Apostle, Therese of Lisiuex, or any of your favorite saints.

> Read books written by saints themselves such as *The Confessions of Saint Augustine*, *The Dark Night of the Soul* (St. John of the Cross), *The Interior Castle* (St. Teresa of Avila), and others.

> Search the Internet for DVDs about the lives of the saints such as *A Man for All Seasons* (St. Thomas More), *Brother Sun, Sister Moon* (St. Francis of Assisi and St. Clare of Assisi), *Joan of Arc*, *John of the Cross*, *Maria Goretti*, and many others.

> Try to become especially familiar with your patron saint (for instance, a saint whose name you share or whom you have chosen to be your special protector, guardian, and source of inspiration).

> Spend a few moments each day learning about the saint of the day (for instance, the saint whose feast is celebrated that day in the Church calendar). Visit www.americancatholic.org/features/saintofday or www.catholic.org/saints/sofd.php.

> Go to http://deepeningfriendship.loyolapress.com/easyquiz/quiz. php?quiz=voices-of-the-saints and take a quiz to find a saint whose life resembles your own. You may learn something new; you may even find a new favorite saint to guide you on your spiritual journey.

Scripture

I am now rejoicing in my sufferings for your sake, and in my flesh I am completing what is lacking in Christ's afflictions for the sake of his body, that is, the church. I became its servant according to God's commission that was given to me for you, to make the word of God fully known, the mystery that has been hidden throughout the ages and generations but has now been revealed to his saints. (COLOSSIANS 1:24–26)

Prayer

Holy Mary, Mother of God *pray for us*

St. Michael,

Holy Angels of God,

St. John the Baptist,

St. Joseph,

St. Peter and St. Paul,

St. Andrew,

St. John,

St. Mary Magdalene,

St. Stephen,

St. Ignatius,

St. Augustine,

St. Francis Xavier,

St. Teresa,

All holy men and women,

(from the Litany of Saints, The Roman Missal)

To share and learn more in a spiritual mentoring relationship about practicing studying the lives of the saints, visit www.loyolapress.com/practice-makes-catholic.

Practice 16

Study Scripture, Tradition, and Catholic Literature

Like all living things, a living faith needs nourishment, which the mature adult disciple finds above all in union with Christ—"the way and the truth and the life" (Jn 14:6). "This life of intimate union with Christ in the Church is maintained by the spiritual helps common to all the faithful, chiefly by active participation in the liturgy." It is also maintained by frequent reading of the word of God, sacred writings of our tradition, and the official documents of the Church. (*Our Hearts Were Burning Within Us*, USCCB, 51)

The Vulcan Mind Meld

Perhaps the most popular character from the world of *Star Trek* was Mr. Spock, the half-human, half-Vulcan first officer of the U.S.S. Enterprise. Among his unique qualities was his ability to perform something called the Vulcan mind meld, which was a technique that Vulcans used to join the mind of another individual to share thoughts, memories, experiences, feelings, and knowledge. In one particular television episode ("Spectre of the Gun," October 25, 1968), Captain Kirk, Dr. McCoy, Mr. Scott, and Mr. Spock find themselves on the wrong end of a re-enactment of the shoot-out at the OK Corral. With his superior intellect, Mr. Spock is able to conclude that the entire experience is an illusion and thus, the bullets cannot harm him. However, he needs to convince his shipmates who, being fully human, suffer the burden of lingering doubt. One by one, Mr. Spock performs mind melds with each of his colleagues, in essence, enabling them to "put on his mind" and dispel all doubt that the bullets are specters that cannot harm them.

St. Paul was not a Vulcan but he understood the concept of a "mind meld" two thousand years before Gene Roddenberry (the creator of *Star Trek*) did. Throughout his letters, St. Paul encourages Christians to put on the mind of Christ as he does here in his letter to the Philippians (2:5): "Let the same mind be in you that was in Christ Jesus."

> **Among the many ways that Catholics attempt to "put on the mind of Christ" is study.**

Among the many ways that Catholics attempt to "put on the mind of Christ," is study. We have already looked at the notion of studying the lives of the saints. Now we turn our attention to three other forms of study that Catholics practice: the study of Scripture, Tradition, and Catholic literature. Through these practices, we seek to put on the mind of Christ.

The Study of Scripture

In her hit song, "One of Us," singer Joan Osborne questioned what it would be like if God was one of us and what it would be like to come face-to-face with him. Catholics believe that God *did* become one of us through the Incarnation and that in Jesus we come face-to-face with God. We also meet God in Scripture as he reveals himself to us through salvation history, culminating in the Word made flesh, Jesus. For Catholics, the study of Scripture is a remarkable way to encounter God.

"I'm looking for my husband. Where's your religion section?"

The bishops of the Second Vatican Council enthusiastically encouraged Catholics to read and study Scripture. In the *Dogmatic Constitution on Divine Revelation* (Dei Verbum), they teach:

> The sacred synod also earnestly and especially urges all the Christian faithful, especially Religious, to learn by frequent reading of the divine Scriptures the "excellent knowledge of Jesus Christ" (Philippians 3:8). "For ignorance of the Scriptures is ignorance of Christ." (25)

For Catholics, the study of Scripture is a remarkable way to encounter God.

When it comes to studying Scripture, Catholics are called to take an intelligent, spiritual approach. Here are ten tips for how to get started with your study of the Bible.

1. Select a Catholic Bible (one that contains all seventy-three books and carries an imprimatur—a declaration from a Catholic bishop assuring that nothing in its contents is contrary to Catholic faith or morals) with a modern translation that reflects the latest in Catholic Scripture scholarship as well as an edition that suits your personal needs for prayer and or study. For a good description of the various translations and editions of the Bible for Catholics, visit http://scriptureschool.org/default.aspx.

2. Read a good introduction to the Bible, such as my book, *The Bible Blueprint: A Catholic's Guide to Understanding and Embracing God's Word* (Loyola Press) or the introductory materials of *The Catholic Study Bible* (Oxford Press) to get basic background on the Bible as well as answers to many common questions.

3. Become familiar with how to use your Bible's study tools most effectively (footnotes, cross-references, commentaries).

4. Consider taking advantage of a resource that has the biblical text and commentary on the same page (such as the *Collegeville Bible Commentary* series) or at least within the same Bible (such as *The Catholic Study Bible*).

5. Begin by reading a part of the Bible that is your favorite or a story/passage that you are familiar with. Consider beginning by reading along with the Church, following the Scripture readings for the Sundays of the Church year, focusing especially on the Gospel. You can find the readings on the Web site of the U.S. Conference of Catholic Bishops: www.usccb.org.

6. Focus on the responsorial psalm for each Sunday as an opportunity to pray with Scripture, making the words of the psalms your own.

7. Eventually, move up to reading an entire book of the Bible. Be sure to read your Bible's introduction to that book in order to get an idea of its background and structure.

8. In the New Testament, consider beginning with the Gospel of Mark (the shortest) or the Gospel currently being used in the Church's cycle of readings. You might also consider starting with the Acts of the Apostles or a New Testament letter such as St. Paul's first letter to the Thessalonians or the letter of James.

> **When we have spiritual reading at meals . . . Christ is there with us.**
> DOROTHY DAY

9. In the Old Testament, consider starting with Exodus 1—20 or the books of Jonah or Ruth, which are compelling, compact stories. If your goal is to deepen your prayer life by using Scripture, consider starting with the Psalms.

10. Wherever you decide to begin, don't rush to get to "the end." Unlike other books, the Bible does not have an ending but rather, invites us to embark on a lifelong journey.

The Study of Tradition

Shouldn't we be able to find everything we need to know about God in the Bible? Well, yes and no. Yes, God has revealed everything we need to know for our salvation through his Son, Jesus. In sacred Scripture, we encounter God's living word. At the same time, the world we live in continues to encounter new challenges, many of which were inconceivable at the time the Bible was written (biblical writings offer no direct comments on issues such as genetic engineering, global warming, and stem-cell research, to name a few). For this reason, God has blessed the Church with a teaching authority: the magisterium (in Latin, the word for teacher or master is *magister*), which is made up of the bishops in communion with the pope under the guidance of the Holy Spirit. We rely on the magisterium to teach authentically and interpret the truths of our faith.

For Catholics, Scripture and Tradition are inseparable, forming one "sacred deposit of the Word of God." (*Catechism of The Catholic Church*, 97) Catholics, in addition to reading and studying Scripture, also read and study Church teachings that come to us through ecumenical councils, papal encyclicals, pastoral letters, and other official sources of teaching from the pope and bishops. Quite often, these documents can be rather dense and require a good deal of unpacking. For

> **It is most common for Catholics to read and study Church documents within the context of a study group.**

this reason, it is most common to read and study Church documents within the context of a study group. Here are some examples of the types of documents we might study:

- **Canons and decrees of the Council of Trent.** Example: *Decree Concerning the Most Holy Sacrament of the Eucharist*

- **Documents of the Second Vatican Council.** Example: *Gaudium et Spes (Pastoral Constitution on the Church in the Modern World)*

- **The *Catechism of the Catholic Church*.** Related resources: *The United States Catholic Catechism for Adults; The Compendium of the Catechism of the Catholic Church*

- **Papal encyclicals (formal letters sent by the pope to clergy and laity to address a particular issue).** Example: *Redemptor Hominis (The Redeemer of Man)*, Pope John Paul II, 1979

- **Apostolic exhortations (communications from the pope that do not define doctrine but rather encourage Catholics to undertake a certain activity. Exhortations are often written in response to a synod of bishops).** Example: *Evangelii Nuntiandi (On Evangelization in the Modern World)*, Pope Paul VI, 1975

- **Pastoral letters issued by a national conference of bishops such as the United States Conference of Catholic Bishops (USCCB).** Example: *Our Hearts Were Burning Within Us : A Pastoral Plan for Adult Faith Formation in the United States* (1999)

> On their way to World Youth Day, two young Catholics decided to study thoroughly the *Catechism of the Catholic Church*. As they came across various references to the devil, one said to the other, "What do you think about all this Satan stuff?" The other replied, "I don't know . . . I think it's like Santa Claus. It's probably just your dad."

The Study of Catholic Literature

At the risk of oversimplifying, let's divide this category into two sections: fiction and nonfiction. Although Catholics do not typically read Church documents as a form of leisure, there are indeed many other examples of Catholic literature that people read at home, at the beach, at the coffee shop, or on the bus. We continue to feed our hunger for God by reading Catholic literature that can be inspirational, catechetical, or both.

Catholics continually strive to feed their hunger for God by reading Catholic literature that can be inspirational, catechetical, or both.

Let's start with Catholic fiction. What exactly makes a piece of literature "Catholic"? The answer to this can be found in part 1 of this book: a sense of sacramentality. Catholic author and sociologist Fr. Andrew Greeley describes it like this:

> Religion . . . is imagination before it's anything else. The Catholic imagination is different from the Protestant imagination. You know that: Flannery O'Connor is not John Updike. The Catholic "classics" assume a God who is present in the world, disclosing Himself in and through creation. The world and all its events, objects, and people tend to be somewhat like God. The Protestant classics, on the other hand, assume a God who is radically absent from the world, and who discloses (Himself) only on rare occasions (especially in Jesus Christ and Him crucified). The world and all its events, objects, and people tend to be radically different from God. (*The Catholic Myth*, Macmillan Publishing Co., 1990, 34–35)

Putting Our Heads Together

For most Catholics, papal encyclicals or other Church documents are not the first choice for reading while relaxing or commuting on the train. However, it is very common to gather in study groups at parishes to study Church documents together. Here is an example from a parish bulletin shortly after Pope Benedict XVI issued his encyclical *Caritas in Veritate*:

> Come and join the Social Ministry Commission for a 4-week group study to learn about Catholic Social Teaching and how it applies to your own life. We will study the last encyclical of Pope Benedict XVI "Caritas in Veritate" released in June 2009. This encyclical is the latest in a series of social encyclicals, shining the light of the Gospel of Christ and the Church's moral teaching on changing social circumstances to provide guidance and support to Christians as we seek to live our faith in the world. For more info and to sign up, contact . . ."

Over the centuries, Catholic authors have found ways of utilizing literature to capture and express this Catholic imagination through fiction. Here are just a few examples of classic Catholic fiction:

- *The Divine Comedy*–Dante
- *The Chronicles of Narnia*–C. S. Lewis
- *The Trees of Pride*–G. K. Chesterton
- *The Power and the Glory*–Graham Greene
- *Mariette in Ecstasy*–Ron Hansen
- *The Violent Bear It Away*–Flannery O'Connor

On to nonfiction. There's an enormous treasury of nonfiction writing from which to draw inspiration. Here are examples of a few timeless Catholic classics of nonfiction:

- *The Imitation of Christ*–Thomas à Kempis
- *The Cloud of Unknowing*–Unknown
- *The Confessions of St. Augustine*–St. Augustine

- **Mere Christianity**–C. S. Lewis
- **The Dark Night of the Soul**–St. John of the Cross
- **The Seven Storey Mountain**–Thomas Merton
- **The Interior Castle**–St. Theresa of Avila
- **Summa Theologica**–St. Thomas Aquinas

Of course, there are plenty of contemporary examples of inspirational Catholic writing; however, to make a list of examples of the "best" would surely stir up a hornet's nest of conflicting opinions from readers. So, instead, I am sharing a totally biased list of some of *my* favorite examples of nonfiction Catholic writing over the past few decades of my life:

- **The Spirit of Early Christian Thought**–Robert Louis Wilken (Yale University Press)
- **The Holy Longing**–Fr. Ronald Rolheiser, OMI (Doubleday)
- **With Open Hands**–Henri Nouwen (Ave Maria Press)
- **The Inner Compass**–Margaret Silf (Loyola Press)
- **The Strangest Way**–Fr. Robert Barron (Orbis Books)
- **Jesus: A Gospel Portrait**–Fr. Donald Senior, CP (Paulist Press)

Enrichment Sounds Better

Personally, when I hear the word *study*, I get flashbacks to my high school and college days when I meticulously pored over notes and textbooks, cramming for exams. When I was introduced, during a Cursillo retreat, to the notion of *study* as a Catholic practice, I didn't exactly jump for joy. However, upon listening to the inspirational talks given on that retreat from fellow Catholics who saw study as a wonderful form of spiritual enrichment, I came to embrace the concept. Over the years, study has enabled me to keep the Lord Jesus on the front burner of my mind where he belongs. With each book I read, I am reminded of how much I do *not* know about God, and how much deeper this knowing can become, if I open up to him and allow him to perform a divine mind meld.

Practical suggestions for practicing study:

> Acquire a Catholic Bible such as the *New American Bible* (the translation used at Mass). Consider the *Catholic Study Bible: New American Bible* (Oxford Press) which provides material for study.

> Select a Catholic Bible commentary (for example, the *Collegeville Bible Commentary*) that meets your needs and that is approved or recommended by your diocesan catechetical office.

> Explore the upcoming Sunday Scripture readings. Visit www.FindingGod.org (Sunday Connection) or www.usccb.org.

> Join a Bible study or Bible discussion group in your parish or in a neighboring Catholic parish.

> Visit Web sites that provide daily reflections on the Scripture readings for Mass such as the daily reflections offered at the United States Conference of Catholic Bishops Web site: www.usccb.org/video /reflections.shtml.

> Visit *Biblia Clerus*, the Web site of the Congregation for the Clergy– www.clerus.org/bibliaclerus–to find reliable materials on the interpretation of Sacred Scripture by the magisterium.

> Regularly acquire and read books and periodicals from Catholic publishers on topics of Scripture, the Mass, spirituality, church history, prayer, and theology. For a list of Catholic publishers, visit www.cbpa.org.

> Join or form a book club to discuss books that add to your spiritual enrichment.

> Visit Catholic Web sites to remain up to date on Church teachings. Begin with your diocesan Web site and search there for reliable links.

> Visit the Vatican Web site–www.vatican.va–to locate documents such as papal encyclicals and the documents of the Second Vatican Council.

> Find church documents at the Theology Library at Spring Hill College (the Jesuit College of the South): www.shc.edu/theolibrary/index.htm.

> Take advantage of learning opportunities offered by your parish or diocese.

> Acquire a copy of the *Compendium of the Catechism of the Catholic Church* or the *United States Catholic Catechism for Adults* to learn more about the Church's official teachings on all aspects of the faith.

Continue on to the *Catechism of the Catholic Church* itself for a more in-depth presentation of the Catholic faith.

> Subscribe to your diocesan newspaper and Catholic magazines.
> Participate in an online study of the Catholic faith such as *Catholic Home Study Service* or *Catholic Information Service* (Knights of Columbus).

Scripture

I will meditate on your precepts,
and fix my eyes on your ways.
I will delight in your statutes;
I will not forget your word.
Deal bountifully with your servant,
so that I may live and observe your word.
Open my eyes, that I may behold
wondrous things out of your law.
(PSALM 119:15–18)

Prayer

Good and gracious God, I want to know you better. You already know me inside and out. Help me come to know you more deeply by learning, reflecting, praying, and studying about all your magnificent ways. Help me put on the mind of your son Jesus Christ, so that I can learn to love as he loved. Amen.

To share and learn more in a spiritual mentoring relationship about practicing studying Scripture, Tradition, and Catholic literature, visit www.loyolapress.com/practice-makes-catholic.

Practice 17

Learn Traditional Prayers

> The memorization of basic prayers offers an essential support to the life of prayer, but it is important to help learners savor their meaning. (*Catechism of the Catholic Church*, 2688)

Family Heirlooms

Most of us have some sort of family heirloom(s). Many of my family heirlooms can be traced back to the family pharmacy that was first owned by my grandfather and then by my dad. When the store closed in 1987, my siblings and I inherited several large apothecary bottles that once actually contained medicine. In a sense, however, these bottles do not belong to us but have been entrusted to us. Our job is to protect them, care for them, tell the stories related to them, and pass them on to future generations of Paprockis.

In essence, this is what we do with our Catholic faith. We're caretakers of a message, one that's not ours but that's been entrusted to us by the Church. Our role is to receive that message, to protect it, to share faithfully the story that lies at the heart of that message, and to transmit that message to the next generation. Among the most precious heirlooms of our Catholic faith are traditional prayers.

In her book *The Words We Pray: Discovering the Richness of Traditional Catholic Prayers* (Loyola Press), author Amy Welborn speaks eloquently of the value of traditional prayers and asserts that "the most important quality of any prayer is that it come from the heart and that it be honest." While it's important for us to be able to speak to God in our own words, traditional prayers offer two critical benefits.

First, we simply cannot count on being able to find the right words with which to pray at any given moment. This is true in our conversations with others, and it's true in our conversations with God. Just think of all the times you have found yourself at a loss for words. Whether it be a moment of overwhelming joy and excitement or devastating loss and sadness, we struggle to express ourselves as we hope to. At moments like these, we are blessed as Catholics to have words provided for us by those whose experience was similar to our own. Whether the words were composed by a saint or by an unknown humble follower of Jesus, traditional prayers can help us express what is in our hearts when our own tongues fall silent.

> **Among the most precious heirlooms of our Catholic faith are traditional prayers.**

Second, traditional prayers connect us with a faith heritage that is deep and rich. Think about it. When we pray traditional prayers, we are forming the same words that were once on the lips of people such as Teresa of Ávila, Ignatius of Loyola, Francis of Assisi, Catherine of Siena, and many other

Memorization: Taking Words to Heart

I grew up in the 1960s, when memorization in education was suddenly looked upon as archaic and ineffective. As a result, I didn't memorize traditional prayers as did previous generations of Catholics. Fast-forward to an adult faith formation session I attended (as part of my role with the Chicago catechetical office), at which forty or fifty senior citizens were participating in a study of the *Catechism*. After I introduced myself, the facilitator invited everyone to join in the Memorare for the opening prayer. There I stood, lip-synching the prayer in front of a room full of fellow Catholics, unable to add my voice to that moment of shared prayer. The truth is, when we memorize—learn "by heart"—the prayers of the Church, we become capable of accessing words that "nourish the human heart and help(s) to form the human spirit in Christ." (*National Directory for Catechesis*, 29F)

Keep the Attitude

The powerful words of the Lord's Prayer, as expressed in Matthew 6:9-13, have been handed on from generation to generation. It is important to know that not only was Jesus teaching words for prayer with the Our Father, he was also teaching an *attitude* for prayer. In teaching the words of this prayer, Jesus teaches us to approach God as we would approach someone with whom we have an intimate relationship. Jesus teaches us to approach God in prayer with an attitude of praise and gratitude, trust and surrender, and of sincere sorrow for our wrongdoings. With this attitude in mind, we can respond to God in prayer in a variety of ways. The traditional prayers of the Church embody all these attitudes.

great saints. Many of us are forming the same words that were once on the lips of our parents, grandparents, and great-grandparents. We are forming the same words that are being spoken by fellow Catholics halfway around the world and in different languages. Traditional prayers remind us that we are not alone; we are members of a community, the Body of Christ. In traditional prayer, we are united in one voice with the communion of saints.

Once again, Amy Welborn says it best when she explains that traditional prayers, "conceived in the womb of God's people, brought to birth, and nurtured by their experiences of hope and faith—are treasures worth rediscovering."

> "Much more is accomplished by a single word of the Our Father said, now and then, from our heart, than by the whole prayer repeated many times in haste and without attention."
>
> St. Teresa of Ávila

When learning how to pray, it's always good to start with what we are most familiar. Most likely you learned traditional prayers in your childhood: the Lord's Prayer, the Hail Mary, and grace at meal times. Traditional prayers are the basic vocabulary of our prayer life. As with all prayer, traditional prayers can be used at any time. You may want to use traditional prayers to help you begin and end your day as well as to mark significant moments in your day such as meals, restful pauses, or moments of solitude.

Practice 17: Learn Traditional Prayers

A mom and dad told their little girl that it was time to go to bed, and they reminded her to kneel down beside her bed and say her prayers before she went to sleep. A few minutes later, they went upstairs to check on her and, sure enough, they saw her kneeling at her bedside with her hands folded, saying the alphabet in the most prayerful manner. They went in and interrupted her saying, "Honey, what are you doing? Don't you remember the prayers that we taught you to say?" The girl said, "I couldn't remember the exact words so I'm just saying all the letters. God knows what I'm thinking and he'll put them all together for me!"

Ten Prayers to Take to Heart

Here is a list of ten prayers that any Catholic would do well to take to heart—which means not only to memorize but also learn the meaning of the words. For the wording of traditional Catholic prayers, visit http://www.loyolapress.com/traditional-catholic-prayers.htm.

- Our Father (the Lord's Prayer)
- Hail Mary
- Glory Be to the Father (Doxology)
- Memorare
- Hail, Holy Queen
- Grace before Meals
- Peace Prayer of Saint Francis of Assisi
- Act of Contrition
- The Guardian Angel Prayer
- The Jesus Prayer

Traditional Formulas of Doctrine

A formula is basically a concise way of expressing some information that provides a solution to a problem. It may also be a statement of a procedure to follow to achieve a solution. Catholics have long embraced formulas of doctrine, taking them to heart as a way of having easy access to the basics of our faith. Being able to recall these formulas enables us to be both concise and precise when speaking about our faith. Traditionally, Catholics are encouraged to take to heart the following formulas of doctrine (for more information on these doctrinal formulas, visit www.loyolapress.com).

- ✚ The Ten Commandments (Exodus 20:1-17)
- ✚ The two commandments of love (Matthew 22:36-39)
- ✚ The Golden Rule (Matthew 7:12)
- ✚ The Beatitudes (Matthew 5:3-12)
- ✚ The theological virtues (1 Corinthians 13:13)
- ✚ The cardinal virtues (Wisdom 8:7)
- ✚ The gifts of the Holy Spirit (Isaiah 11:2-3)
- ✚ The fruits of the Holy Spirit (Galatians 5:22-23)
- ✚ The five precepts of the Church (*Catechism* 2041)
- ✚ The corporal works of mercy (Matthew 25:35-36)
- ✚ The spiritual works of mercy (*Catechism* 2447)
- ✚ The seven deadly (capital) sins (*Catechism* 1866)
- ✚ The four last things (*Catechism* 1020-1041)

> **Catholics have long embraced formulas of doctrine, taking them to heart as a way of having easy access to the basics of our faith.**

The Jesus Prayer

One of the oldest and simplest traditional prayers is known as the Jesus Prayer or the Prayer of the Heart: "Lord Jesus Christ, Son of God, have mercy on me, a sinner."

The words of the prayer are based on the words spoken by two blind men to Jesus in Matthew 20:31 as well as to the tax collector in Luke 18:13. For many Christians, especially in the Eastern Christian traditions, this is a prayer of repetition that leads to stillness of the heart. This short prayer is so power-packed that many see it as a summation of the Christian faith: we proclaim Jesus by name to be the Son of God and the Anointed One (Christ), we proclaim him Lord of our lives, we proclaim his divinity (Son of God), we proclaim him to be in a position of judgment (have mercy), and we proclaim our own sinfulness in need of salvation (a sinner).

Praying Spontaneously: You, Who, Do, Through

In some ways, Catholics' reliance on traditional formulaic prayers has left many of us feeling a bit intimidated by the idea of leading a spontaneous prayer in public. In truth, spontaneous prayer for Catholics also follows a formula to some extent, one we find in the Church's eucharistic prayers. The key words are: *you, who, do, through.*

1. Begin and end with the Sign of the Cross if the gathering is predominantly Catholic.

2. YOU—We begin all our prayers by naming God, who is the *you* upon whom we are calling. We have many different ways to call upon God because God has many divine titles such as, "Heavenly Father," or "Good and Gracious God" or "Almighty and Eternal God."

3. WHO—Next, we recall some of God's great deeds or qualities, reminding ourselves that God has acted first and that our prayer—all prayer—is in response to what God has done for us. For example, we can say something like "You sent your Holy Spirit upon the apostles at Pentecost . . ."

4. DO—We then move from what God has done in the past to pray specifically for what we confidently hope God will do for the people gathered at this moment.

5. THROUGH—Finally, we acknowledge that we come to the Father through his son, Jesus Christ, and by the power of the Holy Spirit, by ending our prayers with words such as "we make this prayer in Jesus' name" or "we ask this through Christ our Lord," or even just the words, "through Christ our Lord."

6. And, don't forget "Amen!"

If you remember these steps and pause briefly between each step, the Holy Spirit will inspire you to find the words to pray spontaneously.

Don't Be Afraid of Doctrine

Most of us live in a culture that emphasizes personal autonomy and does not cultivate respect for authority. As a result, doctrines are unpopular. Some people fear that, by following doctrines, they are losing their own independence. Others feel that doctrine is intended for theologians and not for the average Christian. The fact is, doctrines are designed precisely to help the average Christian have access to the mystery of faith and to avoid false teaching. They help us put into words the unfathomable love of God. Doctrines are not imposed upon us but are embraced by us in baptism and confirmation. Doctrine provides a vision for life. By taking to heart doctrinal formulas, we enable ourselves to encounter Jesus, who is the Way, the Truth, and the Life.

Practical suggestions for practicing traditional prayers and doctrinal formulas:

> Over time, take to heart (memorize) traditional prayers such as those provided in this section.

> Learn about the background of traditional prayers from a resource such as *The Words We Pray: Discovering the Richness of Traditional Catholic Prayers*, Amy Welborn, (Loyola Press).

> Visit www.FindingGod.org (Resources/Prayer and Spirituality/ Traditional Catholic Prayers) for the wording of numerous traditional prayers.

> Include a traditional prayer as you begin and end your day and at significant moments throughout your day such as mealtimes, moments of pause or solitude, or challenges such as meetings, exams, important encounters, travel, and so on.

> Include a traditional prayer if called upon to lead a group in prayer.

> Take to heart (memorize) traditional prayers and/or doctrinal formulas during your commute or while exercising.

> Use the season of Lent to take to heart (memorize) traditional prayers and/or doctrinal formulas.

- > Learn to pray traditional prayerful devotions such as the Rosary or the Way of the Cross. Visit www.FindingGod.org.
- > Learn the Latin versions of some traditional prayers such as the Signum Crucis (Sign of the Cross), Pater Noster (Our Father), Ave Maria (Hail Mary), Gloria Patri (Glory Be), Salve Regina (Hail Holy Queen). Visit http://www.loyolapress.com/traditional-catholic-prayers-in-latin.htm.
- > Occasionally volunteer to pray spontaneously at gatherings of family, friends, fellow parishioners, and so on.

Scripture

Pray then this way: Our Father in heaven,
hallowed be your name.
Your kingdom come.
Your will be done,
on earth as it is in heaven.
Give us this day our daily bread;
And forgive us our debts,
as we also have forgiven our debtors.
And do not bring us to the time of trial,
but rescue us from the evil one.
(MATTHEW 6:9–13, RSV)

Prayer

O my God, I am heartily sorry for having offended Thee and I detest all my sins because of thy just punishments, but most of all because they offend Thee, my God, who art all good and deserving of all my love. I firmly resolve, with the help of Thy grace, to sin no more and to avoid the near occasion of sin. Amen.

To share and learn more in a spiritual mentoring relationship about practicing traditional prayers and doctrinal formulas, visit www.loyolapress.com/practice-makes-catholic.

PART FIVE

AN ATTITUDE OF FAITH AND HOPE

Catholics are a people of the Resurrection, which means that, deep down, we recognize that we have no reason to despair because God has shown that he can overcome all things, even death. Catholics are a people of hope. We see the world as good. We have a positive vision, fueled by our belief that God loves us so much, that he gave us his only Son, who is with us always through the Holy Spirit. This worldview calls us to be evangelizers, eagerly proclaiming the good news of Jesus to others in word and deed.

And so we have a disposition of faith and hope and not despair. We are not doomsayers. By the same token, we do not see the world through rose-colored glasses. We are realists. We see, feel, and experience pain, violence, sadness, hurt, and evil. However, our faith teaches us that God will overcome all and that we are not alone. That's not simply being optimistic or engaging in wishful thinking. This is a disposition of confidence. We have every reason to believe, every reason to hope, and, when all is said and done, no reason to despair.

In part five, we'll look at the following Catholic practices related to our disposition of faith and hope and not despair:

Practice 18: Adjust Your Attitude

Practice 19: Comfort One Another

Practice 20: Keep a Song in Your Heart

Practice 21: Make a Retreat

To share and learn more in a spiritual mentoring relationship about practicing the Catholic disposition of faith and hope, visit www.loyolapress.com/practice-makes-catholic.

Practice 18

Adjust Your Attitude

Faith, hope and charity go together. Hope is practiced through the virtue of patience. . . . Faith tells us that God has given his Son for our sakes and gives us the victorious certainty that it is really true: God is love! Love is the light—and in the end, the only light—that can always illuminate a world grown dim and give us the courage needed to keep living and working. (*God Is Love*, Pope Benedict XVI, 2005)

That Certain Something

In his song, "Something," Beatles member George Harrison described the intangible qualities that he saw in his lover: "Something in the way she moves, attracts me like no other lover." Well, there is "something" about the way followers of Jesus conduct themselves that attracts other people to want to become disciples themselves. In fact, a great Church father, Tertullian (about AD 200), quoted non-Christians as saying about Jesus' followers: "See how they love one another." And Jesus told his disciples, "By this everyone will know that you are my disciples, if you have love for one another" (John 13:35). As we go about our daily lives, we are called to do so in an attitude that expresses faith and hope, an attitude that dispels the darkness. Catholicism provides three formulas that summarize what this attitude or, disposition, looks like. These are the fruits of the Holy Spirit, the theological virtues, and the Beatitudes;

they outline the qualities that, through the Holy Spirit's presence in our lives, give us a certain "something."

Spiritually Inebriated: The Fruits of the Spirit

When people consume alcohol, the effects are noticeable. Moderate drinking results in a lightened mood, a tendency toward giddiness, a loss of inhibition, a decrease in motor ability, and an increase in conversation. The effects of a different kind of spirit are also noticeable. When we "drink" of the Holy Spirit of Jesus Christ, there is a distinct increase in the following: love, faithfulness, joy, modesty, kindness, goodness, peace, patience, self-control, chastity, generosity, gentleness.

It is no coincidence that, when the crowds saw the apostles after they had been filled with the Holy Spirit on Pentecost, they concluded that the apostles were drunk.

> Like solid objects displacing water in a glass, the fruits of the Holy Spirit leave little room for anger, despair, envy, jealousy, sadness, and hatred.

People who are filled with the Holy Spirit exhibit tendencies that are the result—the fruits—of the Holy Spirit's presence. Like the wind that is invisible and noticed only by its effects on swaying branches and swirling

Who Makes Up These Things?

The fruits of the Holy Spirit were not simply concocted by Vatican officials to give Catholics another list to memorize. In fact, these fruits are based on a passage from St. Paul's letter to the Galatians:

> By contrast, the fruit of the Spirit is love, joy, peace, patience, kindness, generosity, faithfulness, gentleness, and self-control. There is no law against such things. And those who belong to Christ Jesus have crucified the flesh with its passions and desires. (Galatians 5:22-24)

The Catholic Church includes three other fruits—generosity, modesty, and chastity—which were originally included in the Latin Vulgate Bible but were omitted from several Greek and Latin manuscripts.

> A Catholic man was trying to impart his confident and hopeful attitude to a very negative friend who was impressed by nothing. It so happened that the Catholic man owned a dog that could walk on water. So he took his negative friend down to the lake, threw a stick into the water, and told his dog to go fetch. Sure enough, the dog walked across the water, retrieved the floating stick, and walked back across the water. The Catholic man said, "So, did you notice something unusual about my dog?" to which his negative friend replied, "I sure did. The poor thing can't swim."

leaves, the Holy Spirit is invisible but is evidenced by its effects on people. In the sacrament of baptism, we receive the Holy Spirit. This "drinking in" of the Spirit produces an increase in divine qualities. Like solid objects displacing water in a glass, the fruits of the Holy Spirit leave little room for anger, despair, envy, jealousy, sadness, and hatred. When we practice the fruits of the Holy Spirit, we acknowledge the gift of the Spirit's presence in our lives. The Spirit is forever prompting us to exhibit these fruits. When we do so, we are responding to the invitation to be more like Christ.

Factory-Equipped: The Theological Virtues

When buying a car, it's good to know what comes as standard equipment—that is, factory equipped. The more features that come factory-equipped, the better the value. As human beings made in the image and likeness of God, we come "factory-equipped" with three very valuable resources: the virtues of faith, hope, and charity (love).

Virtues are gifts from God that lead us to live in a close relationship with him. Virtues are like habits: they need to be practiced, and they can be lost if they are neglected. The virtues of faith, hope, and charity

> **Virtues are gifts from God that lead us to live in a close relationship with him.**

are not "add-ons" that we acquire if we're interested. They come from God and are part of the package he provides so that we can live in relationship with him and with one another. Because these virtues come from God, we call them the theological virtues. Like any gift, God intends that we use them not only for our own welfare, but also for the welfare of others.

Faith is our trust and belief in God that dispels fear. We profess our faith in the creed, celebrate it in the sacraments, live by it through our good conduct of loving God and our neighbor, and express it in prayer.

Hope is the confidence that God will always be with us. It is our confidence that God has a plan for us to enjoy fullness of life now and forever.

Charity is the love we have for God, expressed through love for neighbor. Love is not a warm and fuzzy feeling. It is a decision, a commitment to the well-being of others, even at our own expense.

A Recipe for Happiness: The Beatitudes

Most people want to be happy. The problem is, happiness is fleeting. And unfortunately, we tend to confuse happiness with joy. Happiness is an emotion that comes and goes. Joy is a deep gladness that persists even in times of sorrow. It's not normal to be happy when a loved one dies. For a Christian, however, it is possible to experience joy even in the midst of grieving. Jesus came that we might have joy; he didn't come to make us happy.

With that in mind, we may find it strange that many English translations of the Bible have Jesus using the word "happy" in the Beatitudes ("Happy are the poor in spirit . . .") In fact, the first word used in each Beatitude in the Greek text is *makarios* which means "happy" or "blessed (blest)." The Greek word conveys deep joy that comes from serving God's kingdom and having a positive direction for our lives. The Beatitudes, then, describe to us what it means to belong to God's kingdom. They are a recipe for true happiness, the kind

> **"Hope is patience with the lamp lit."**
> TERTULLIAN

The Inner Commandments

While the majority of the Ten Commandments describe external actions that we need to avoid and are stated negatively, the Beatitudes are concerned with inner realities and are stated positively.

> Blessed are the poor in spirit, for theirs is the kingdom of heaven.
> Blessed are those who mourn, for they will be comforted.
> Blessed are the meek, for they will inherit the earth.
> Blessed are those who hunger and thirst for righteousness, for they wiill be filled.
> Blessed are the merciful, for they will receive mercy.
> Blessed are the pure in heart, for they will see God.
> Blessed are the peacemakers, for they will be called children of God.
> Blessed are those who are persecuted for righteousness' sake, for theirs is the kingdom of heaven.
> Blessed are you when people revile you and persecute you and utter all kinds of evil against you falsely on my account. Rejoice and be glad, for your reward is great in heaven, for in the same way they persecuted the prophets who were before you. (Matthew 5:3-12)

found not by those who have riches, or power, or popularity, or comfortable lives, but by those who are poor in spirit or who mourn or who are merciful. The Beatitudes teach us that God's grace and doing God's will are the only means to true happiness or joy. The Beatitudes are a mindset, a way to see life as God sees life: a *blest* way to see.

Practical suggestions for practicing the fruits of the Holy Spirit, the theological virtues, and the Beatitudes:

Fruits of the Holy Spirit

> **Love**—Seek to show love in selfless service to others by words and actions.

> **Faithfulness**—Keep your promises and show loyalty to God and to those to whom you have made commitments.

> **Joy**—Express a deep and constant gladness in God that circumstances cannot destroy.

> **Modesty**—Express moderation in all your actions, especially your conversations and external behavior, including how you dress.

> **Kindness**—Show kindness by generous acts of service.

> **Goodness**—Try to love all people without exception and to do good to them.

> **Peace**—Commit yourself to being serene, not overly anxious or upset.

> **Patience**—Show that you are willing to endure life's suffering, difficulties, and routine and that you are not going to give up in difficult situations.

> **Self-control**—Discipline your physical and emotional desires by being modest and respectful of others.

> **Chastity**—Commit to an ongoing integration of your physical sexuality with your spiritual nature.

> **Generosity**—Show that you are willing to give to others, even at a cost to yourself.

> **Gentleness**—Show that your strength is tempered by love; learn to forgive instead of getting angry.

Theological Virtues

> Begin each day by placing your trust in God: Father, Son, and Holy Spirit.

> Try each day to live with the confidence, conviction, and courage that comes from faith.

> Live without fear and help dispel fear from the lives of others.

> At work, home, and play express optimism grounded in the virtue of hope.

> Respond to those who are cynical or despairing with a message of confident hope.

> Use the gift of hope to be the voice of reason, assurance, and perspective, especially for those who have lost their sense of perspective.

> Live with a charitable attitude toward all those you encounter, showing concern for their well-being.

> Combine your acts of charity with prayers for the well-being of the recipients of that charity.

> Show charity to your enemies; commit yourself to the well-being of those you think of as enemies.

Beatitudes

> *Blessed are the poor in spirit* . . . live with a detachment from material goods and an attitude of gratitude for all you have.

> *Blessed are those who mourn* . . . be sorrowful for your sins and for the sins and injustices of society, and allow your mourning to lead to repentance.

> *Blessed are the meek* . . . show restraint, be gentle of spirit but strong in commitment.

> *Blessed are they who hunger and thirst for righteousness* . . . desire what is just, show compassion and mercy for all, respect people's rights, fulfill your obligations to others, and care for those who are in need.

> *Blessed are the merciful* . . . give others more love than they deserve; offer people who have wronged you another chance; be a forgiving person; let go of grudges.

> *Blessed are the pure in heart* . . . remain focused on the Gospel and on your mission as a disciple of Jesus; avoid distractions but stay focused on God.

> *Blessed are the peacemakers* . . . offer to resolve conflicts at work and at home; help reconcile people to one another.

> *Blessed are those who are persecuted righteousness' sake* . . . take pleasure only in knowing that you are doing God's will.

> *Blessed are you when people revile you and persecute you and utter all kinds of evil against you falsely on my account* . . . know that, even when it seems that no one else appreciates you, God loves you; know that following Jesus means following him to the cross.

Scripture

Rejoice in the Lord always; again I will say, Rejoice. Let your gentleness be known to everyone. The Lord is near. Do not worry about anything, but in everything by prayer and supplication with thanksgiving let your requests be made known to God. And the peace of God, which surpasses all understanding, will guard your hearts and your minds in Christ Jesus. (PHILIPPIANS 4:4–7)

Prayer

Heavenly Father, send forth the Holy Spirit so that my life will bear the Spirit's fruit. Help me give evidence of your Spirit's presence through my words and deeds, even my attitude. Strengthen me in faith, hope, and love, so that I will trust in the cross of your son, Jesus, that I will be anchored in the life of the Trinity, and that my heart will be on fire with love for you. Help me live the Beatitudes so that I will know what it means to be truly happy, truly blessed. Amen.

To share and learn more in a spiritual mentoring relationship about practicing the fruits of the Spirit, the theological virtues, and the Beatitudes, visit www.loyolapress.com/practice-makes-catholic.

Practice 19

Comfort One Another

There is nothing more man needs than Divine Mercy—that love which is benevolent, which is compassionate, which raises man above his weakness to the infinite heights to the holiness of God. (Pope John Paul II at the Shrine of Divine Mercy in Cracow, Poland, on June 7, 1999)

Begging for Mercy

When we think of the word *mercy*, we often picture someone groveling at the feet of some violent, cruel, and ruthless villain, pleading for his or her life to be spared. When we ask God for mercy, on the other hand, we are not doing so because we are fearful of incurring some violent punishment or retribution for our sins. Rather, we are calling on God in the only way we know God—as merciful, as one who responds with compassion to the needs of those who are suffering. We have done nothing to deserve this mercy. It is only through God's freely given compassion and mercy that we are saved.

We, in turn, are called to be merciful to others. In Luke's Gospel we hear Jesus say, "Be merciful, just as your Father is merciful" (Luke 6:36). This means that we are to respond to those who are suffering as God does: with compassion. The Church teaches works of mercy that serve not only the physical needs of others (the corporal works of mercy) but also their spiritual needs—the spiritual works of mercy.

The *Catechism of the Catholic Church* teaches that "The desire for God is written in the human heart" (27) and that "desire for true happiness frees man from his immoderate attachment to the goods of this world so that he can find his fulfillment in the vision and beatitude of God." (2548) The spiritual works of mercy, then, are ways in which we help others find fulfillment—true happiness—by removing obstacles or helping people overcome them. The Church names the spiritual works of mercy as: instructing, advising, consoling, comforting, forgiving, bearing wrongs patiently, and praying for the living and the dead.

Since the spiritual works of mercy are concrete actions that embody our disposition of faith and hope and not despair,

> ## The Source, of Course
>
> Unlike the corporal works of mercy, which are traced to Matthew 25, the spiritual works of mercy are not drawn from a single Scripture passage but from a variety of them, in both the Old and New Testaments:
>
> - > Instructing: Colossians 3:16
> - > Advising: Galatians 6:1; Jude 1:23
> - > Consoling: John 14:27
> - > Comforting: Isaiah 66:13; Galatians 6:2
> - > Bearing Wrongs Patiently/ Forgiving: Colossians 3:12
> - > Praying for the Living and the Dead: Ephesians 6:18

I thought it would be best to cover each of them by providing real-life examples of Catholics whose lives and actions exemplify these works.

Instructing

In the Gospel of Matthew, Jesus' last words before his ascension into heaven are, "Go therefore and make disciples of all nations, baptizing them in the name of the Father and of the Son and of the Holy Spirit, *and teaching* them to obey everything that I have commanded you. And remember, I am with you always, to the end of the age." (Matthew 28:19–20, emphasis added). Since that moment, Christians have been teaching—instructing—others who have not yet heard the good news of Jesus. We ourselves are called to be open to instruction so that we can continue deepening our relationship with God. Then, in our roles as parents, godparents, sponsors, catechists, friends, and neighbors, we instruct others.

One of the best examples of Catholics dedicated to instructing others is St. Katharine Drexel, born in 1858 into a prominent and wealthy family in Philadelphia. She was instructed well in the Catholic faith and developed a deep and loving relationship with God. She took great interest in serving the needs of people of color, especially African-Americans and Native Americans. Eventually she founded a religious community, the Sisters of the Blessed Sacrament, working and praying tirelessly until her death in 1955. She established sixty-three schools throughout the country, including Xavier University in New Orleans. Along the way, Katharine dedicated $20 million of her own money to these efforts. Because of her lifelong dedication to this spiritual work of mercy, Pope John Paul II canonized her on October 1, 2000, making her the second American-born saint.

Advising

This spiritual work of mercy is sometimes referred to as "admonish the sinner" and refers to our responsibility to correct behavior that goes against God's will. Easier said than done, especially in today's society in which people don't like being told what they can or cannot do. Whenever we advise or admonish, we are immediately accused of judging others. However, advising or admonishing the sinner is not about passing judgment but is a fraternal correction that is an act of love, not of condemnation. The goal of fraternal correction is not to humiliate or destroy the person you're correcting; the goal is helping that person restore relationship with God and others through right behavior.

A good example of this spiritual work of mercy is Deacon John Green, founder of Emmaus Ministries. This ministry works with young adult homeless men involved in prostitution. After years of traveling several nights a week from his home in the western suburbs of Chicago into the city, reaching out to hustlers, Green founded Emmaus Ministries in 1990. Today, fourteen staff and thirty-five volunteers participate in nightly outreach to male prostitutes in the Chicago area. The goal of this ministry is to change the lives of these sexually exploited men. Anyone could rant and rave about the evils of

> "Extend your mercy towards others, so that there can be no one in need whom you meet without helping. For what hope is there for us if God should withdraw His Mercy from us?"
> SAINT VINCENT DE PAUL

prostitution. Anyone could easily condemn the actions of those involved in male prostitution. Deacon Green has chosen instead to embody one of the spiritual works of mercy—advising (admonishing the sinner)—as a means of bringing about the true conversion and transformation for men trapped in a destructive way of life.

Consoling

Thomas the Apostle is not alone in being a doubter. We all doubt from time to time. We live in a world that surrounds us with doubt. One of the spiritual works of mercy—consoling or counseling the doubtful—calls us to help others overcome doubt and live in hope. Although doubt is a normal human emotion, it can prevent the growth of healthy faith. Faith leaves room for curiosity and seeking, but it leaves no room for the questioning of revealed truth. As people of faith, we are called to help those who are experiencing doubt because they have yet to embrace the sure hope of salvation in Jesus Christ.

A great example of this spiritual work of mercy is St. Marcellin Champagnat, the founder of the Marist Brothers. Born in France in 1789, Marcellin grew up in a small hamlet that suffered through the turmoil of the French Revolution. While studying in the seminary, he came up with the idea of forming a religious order to work with children living in remote rural areas who had been deprived of Christian education. After his ordination as a priest, Marcellin began serving the needs of people who did not have access to a quality education. When ministering to a seventeen-year-old boy who was dying, Marcellin was distressed to learn that the boy

A young Catholic missionary serving in a non-Christian foreign country angered the country's dictator by empowering the poor and oppressed to rise up in revolt. The dictator had the missionary arrested and sentenced to death. The missionary's community pleaded with the dictator for mercy. In a mocking gesture of mercy, the dictator announced that he would allow the missionary to choose how he would like to die. Standing before the dictator, the missionary said, "Thank you, Sir, for this generous show of mercy. Given my choice of how to die, I choose to die of old age."

knew none of the basic beliefs of the Catholic Church. In 1817, he founded the Marist Brothers, who set out to teach the basics of the faith along with reading and writing to those who were most neglected, thus bringing hope to many people who lived in despair. Today, nearly four thousand Marist Brothers continue Marcellin's ministry of educating young people all over the world, and dispelling the doubt that comes with a lack of education and religious formation.

Comforting

In 1992, the rock group R.E.M. hit the charts with their song "Everybody Hurts," a song that resonated with people around the world. Indeed, everybody hurts. Which means that everybody, at one time or other, needs comfort. Comforting the sorrowful is one of the spiritual works of mercy, calling us to reach out to those who are suffering. By doing so, we help them see how their suffering can be united with the suffering of Jesus and, eventually, transformed. At the very least, we remind them that they are not alone or abandoned.

Perhaps the most well-known example in recent times of someone who comforted the sorrowful is Blessed Mother Teresa of Calcutta, the tiny woman who worked among the poorest of the poor in India. While teaching high school in India as a Loreto Sister, Theresa found that she could not ignore the dire poverty that surrounded her. She felt a call to "follow Christ into the slums to serve him among the poorest of the poor." In 1950, Mother Teresa founded the Missionaries of Charity and lived the rest of her life in the slums of Calcutta, comforting and caring for those who were dying, orphans, abandoned children, the aging, street people, and alcoholics. She joyfully and tirelessly performed this spiritual work of mercy until her death in 1997. She was beatified by Pope John Paul II in 2003.

Bearing Wrongs Patiently

The late comedian George Carlin joked about how we commonly refer to anyone driving slower than us as "an idiot" and anyone driving faster than us as "a maniac!" It is sadly true that driving often brings out the worst in us. The spiritual work of mercy—bearing wrongs patiently—calls us to take a deep breath when we are wronged by others. This patient pause is often the prerequisite to other spiritual works of mercy, such as admonishing the sinner (in a loving way) and forgiving. Suffering wrongs patiently is not to be confused with accepting evil. Rather, it is a crucial step in trusting that ultimately justice rests in God's hands. There is only so much we can do right here and right now. In bearing wrongs patiently, we adamantly hold on to hope.

Fr. Martin Lawrence Jenco is a good example of this spiritual work of mercy. Fr. Jenco, a priest from Joliet, Illinois, was taken hostage in Beirut, where he was serving as director of Catholic Relief Services. He was held hostage for 564 days, during which time he was often chained and blindfolded. He patiently endured, passing the time by praying and meditating, celebrating Mass when possible, and making a Rosary out of loose threads from a sack. After his release, Fr. Jenco wrote a book, *Bound to Forgive*, in which he described his efforts to bear patiently the wrong that was being done to him, something that enabled him eventually to let go of revenge and forgive his captors.

Forgiving

The day before I wrote this particular section of this book, a controversial play happened in a Major League Baseball game. Detroit Tigers pitcher Armando Galarraga was pitching a perfect game with only one out to go when he covered first base on a ground ball and obviously stepped on the bag a moment before the runner. However, umpire Jim Joyce called the runner safe, thus squelching the possibility of a no-hitter/perfect game. Replays clearly showed the runner was out by a full step. After initially expressing some bitterness, Galaragga accepted the apology of umpire Joyce, who admitted to blowing the call. The next day, the two embraced at home plate in a profound display of reconciliation. To forgive injuries is a spiritual work of mercy that does not come easy to any of us, thus, the saying, "to err is human, to forgive is divine." Forgiveness runs contrary to our human impulses. Yet forgiveness is at the very heart of God's love for us.

"Your Honor, we find the defendant guilty but forgiven."

An example of the spiritual work of mercy—forgiving injuries—is Pope John Paul II, who saw fit to forgive the man who tried to assassinate him. In 1981, as his motorcade made it slowly through St. Peter's Square, Pope John Paul II was felled and critically wounded by several bullets from the gun of would-be assassin Mehmet Ali Agca, a Turk. Agca was captured and sent to prison, and Pope John Paul II recovered. In 1983, the pope visited Agca in his jail cell and, in a twenty-minute meeting, forgave him, grasping the hand by which, just two years before, Agca had fired the shot that nearly ended the pope's life.

Praying for the Living and the Dead

When elderly Jesuit priests and brothers go to live at the Columbiere Jesuit Center, it is not announced as a retirement but as a new assignment: to pray for the Church and the Society. In other words, although these Jesuits may not be able to participate in some of the other ministries of the Society due to age or health, they are still able to participate in an important ministry of the Church: praying for others. This spiritual work of mercy has deep roots in our Judeo-Christian history and in Scripture (for example: 1 Samuel 12:19, 23; Psalm 122:9; James 5:16; John 17:9). Praying on behalf of and in remembrance of others is an expression of faith, hope, and charity.

Teresa of Ávila is a good example of someone who practiced this spiritual work of mercy. Because of the restrictions placed on women in society, Teresa felt that the most useful thing she could do for the Church was to pray for its needs. She founded many monasteries, the first of which was St. Joseph's Monastery in 1562, where "the business of the community was prayer and prayer was its language." To this day, the Discalced (Barefoot) Carmelites are dedicated to a life of prayer in service to the Church.

Practical suggestions for practicing the spiritual works of mercy:

> **Instructing**—commit yourself to learning about the Catholic faith and share your understanding of the faith with your children and with those who welcome it; share your insights, knowledge, and skills with others, especially coworkers; take time to "tutor" those who are just beginning tasks such as parenting or a new job; read good literature and encourage others to do the same.

> **Advising**—be courageous yet compassionate in calling people and institutions to be faithful to Gospel values; intervene in situations in which people are clearly doing harm to themselves or others; respond to negative and prejudicial comments with positive statements; put an end to gossip by walking away; set a good example for others.

> **Consoling**—work at being optimistic and avoiding cynicism; respond to cynicism, skepticism, and doubt with hope; be articulate about your own hopes; ask people about their hopes and support them in trying to attain them.

> **Comforting**—walk with others through their pain; offer words of encouragement to those who seem discouraged; offer positive words to coworkers who are having a difficult time with their tasks; be present to those who are struggling or in emotional pain or despair; offer sympathy to those who are grieving.

> **Bearing wrongs patiently**—work at being less critical of others; overlook minor flaws and mistakes; give people the benefit of the doubt; assume that people who may have hurt you did so because they are enduring pain of their own; pray for those who have wronged you.

> **Forgiving**—pray for those who have wronged you and pray for the courage to forgive; ask forgiveness from others; let go of grudges; go out of your way to be positive with someone you are having a difficult time with.

> **Praying for the living and the dead**—when someone confides in you about a burden, assure them of your prayers; begin and end your day by offering prayers for those in need and for those who have died; when you pray the "Hail Mary," say, "Holy Mary, Mother of God, pray for . . . (and mention the names of those for whom you wish to pray) . . . and for all of us sinners, now and at the hour of our death. Amen."

Scripture

My friends, if anyone is detected in a transgression, you who have received the Spirit should restore such a one in a spirit of gentleness. Take care that you yourselves are not tempted. Bear one another's burdens, and in this way you will fulfil the law of Christ. So let us not grow weary in doing what is right, for we will reap at harvest time, if we do not give up. So then, whenever we have an opportunity, let us work for the good of all, and especially for those of the family of faith. (GALATIANS 6:1–2, 9–10)

Prayer

Lord, God, you always show me your great mercy. Help me share your mercy with others through the spiritual works of mercy. Through my actions, may I help others overcome spiritual obstacles and find fulfillment—true happiness—in you. Help me instruct, advise, console, comfort, forgive, bear wrongs patiently, and pray for the living and the dead. Amen.

To share and learn more in a spiritual mentoring relationship about practicing the spiritual works of mercy, visit www.loyolapress.com/practice-makes-catholic.

Practice 20

Keep a Song in Your Heart

One cannot find anything more religious and more joyful in sacred celebrations than a whole congregation expressing its faith and devotion in song. Therefore the active participation of the whole people, which is shown in singing, is to be carefully promoted. . . . (*Musicam Sacram: Instruction on Music in the Liturgy, 16, Sacred Congregation of Rites*)

Lift Up Your Hearts

Imagine a birthday party with all the expected hoopla: cake, candles, decorations, presents, party hats, and so on. Everyone gathers around the person of honor who sits gleefully in front of a birthday cake full of lit candles. Someone steps forward and says, "Due to time constraints, we won't be able to *sing* Happy Birthday, let's just recite the words." The crowd then *recites* the following words:

Happy birthday to you. Happy birthday to you. Happy birthday dear _____. Happy birthday to you.

This would probably be followed by the sound of crickets chirping!

Everyone knows that "Happy Birthday" must be sung! It is only when these words are joyfully sung that the person of honor may be brought to tears of joy. Singing has that power. Think of how powerfully songs from famous musicals can evoke emotion from listeners. When words are put to melody and sung with feeling, a different part of the human spirit is touched.

Singing enjoys a very prominent role in Catholic life. In the Mass, the priest calls us to lift up our hearts, an act that is aided by singing. At Mass, in addition to the hymns we sing, we also sing many of the prayers and Mass parts. All these moments of singing express our faith and, at the same time, shape and form us as people of faith.

In our individual prayer lives, song can play a prominent role, whether we are listening to recordings of sacred hymns, singing them out loud, or just singing them silently in our minds. The beauty of these sacred hymns is that they also teach. The lyrics to sacred hymns articulate our most sacred beliefs. No doubt, if some society were to ban all copies of the *Catechism of the Catholic Church* as well as all textbooks that teach the Catholic faith, people would still be able to learn about the Catholic faith if the only book left to them was a hymnal. A real-life example of this was witnessed in Poland during the last century. Although persecuted by communism and prevented from using textbooks to teach the Catholic faith, the Church in Poland not only survived but thrived by passing along the faith from one generation to the next in song.

> **Singing enjoys a very prominent role in Catholic life.**

St. Augustine taught that when we sing, we pray twice. I can think of no better way to lift up our hearts!

Through Hymns, with Hymns, and in Hymns

The *Catechism of the Catholic Church* tells us that "The desire for God is written in the human heart" (27). So just what is the way to a person's heart? Aside from the popular notion that the way to a man's heart is through his stomach, Catholics recognize that, in order to penetrate the human heart where the desire for God resides, words alone (and food) do not suffice.

"The sopranos and altos will sing, 'Hallelujah,' the tenors will sing, 'Amen,' and the basses will sing, 'Oo-waw, diddle-dee, doo waw.'"

The Daddy of All Musicians

Music is so important in salvation history that the book of Genesis tells us that one of Adam's grandsons was named Jubal (a name which means *horn*, from which we get the word *jubilee*) who was considered the ancestor of all who play the lyre and harp (Genesis 4:21). In a similar way, the Bible "ends" in the book of Revelation with the sound of a trumpet signaling the end of the world (Revelation 11:15) and the Church singing a victory song (Revelation 19:5-10). References to singing and music occur more than three hundred times throughout the Bible.

The language of mystery requires more than words. Music, therefore, is one of the most powerful elements of the language of mystery. It is absolutely unthinkable to conceive of the Catholic faith without music and singing. For this reason, Catholics recognize the crucial role that music and song play in our faith formation. To this end, I have put together a "musical curriculum" of the Catholic faith.

I call this the "soundtrack to the *Catechism*." By drawing on both traditional and contemporary church hymns, we can come into contact with the central teachings of the Catholic faith while raising our minds, hearts, and voices to God.

St. Augustine taught that when we sing, we pray twice.

Part One: Profession of Faith

Part One, the longest of the four parts of the *Catechism*, deals with the longing that human beings have for God and how God responds to that desire by revealing himself to us. Jesus, of course, is the pinnacle of that revelation. Jesus, in turn, transmitted the truths of divine revelation to his apostles and, through them, to the Church. The greatest part of Part One is devoted to the Creed—our profession of faith in the Father, the Son, the Holy Spirit, and the Church, including Mary and the saints. Some hymns that reflect the theology of Part One of the *Catechism* include:

How Great Thou Art
I Have Loved You
Your Word Is My Light
Sow the Word
Here I Am, Lord
Now Thank We All,
    Our God
I Say Yes
We Walk by Faith
Holy God, We Praise Thy
    Name
O God, Almighty Father
All Hail, Adored Trinity
Morning Has Broken
All Creatures of Our God and
    King
Jesus, the Lord
To Jesus Christ, Our
    Sovereign King
Come All Ye Faithful
Were You There?
O Sacred Head Surrounded
Behold the Wood
Lift High the Cross
Sing My Tongue

Ye Sons and Daughters
Jesus Christ Is Risen Today
Crown Him with Many Crowns
Soon and Very Soon
Come, O Come, Emmanuel
Come Holy Ghost
Veni Sancti Spiritus
Veni Creator Spiritus
O Holy Spirit by Whose
    Breath
Gather Us In
All Are Welcome
One Bread, One Body
The Church's One Foundation
We Are Many Parts
Sing of Mary
Immaculate Mary
Hail, Holy Queen
Ave Maria
Salve Regina
At the Cross Her Station
    Keeping (Stabat Mater)
Hail Mary, Gentle Woman
For All the Saints

The Sunday before Christmas, a pastor told his congregation that the church needed some extra money. He asked the people to consider donating a little more than usual into the collection. He said that whoever gave the most would be able to pick out three hymns for Christmas. After the collection was taken up, the pastor glanced down and noticed that someone had donated a $1,000 bill. He was so excited that he immediately shared his joy with his congregation and said he'd like to personally thank the person who placed the money in the collection. A very quiet, elderly, saintly looking lady all the way in the back shyly raised her hand. The pastor asked her to come to the front. Slowly she made her way to the pastor. He told her how wonderful it was that she gave so much and in thanks asked her to pick out three hymns for Christmas. Her eyes brightened as she looked over the congregation, pointed to the three most handsome men in the building and said, "I'll take him and him and him."

Part Two: Celebration of the Christian Mystery

The second pillar of the *Catechism* is primarily concerned with the liturgy of the Church (signs and symbols, words and actions, singing and music, the liturgical calendar, and so on). This section then goes on to deal with each of the seven sacraments of the Church. Some hymns that reflect the theology of Part Two of the *Catechism* include:

At That First Eucharist
We Remember
This is the Feast of Victory
Litany of Saints
Baptized in Water
Healing River
Come to the Water
Amazing Grace
Here I Am, Lord
Send Us Your Spirit
You Have Anointed Me

O Holy Spirit By Whose Breath
Be Not Afraid
On Eagle's Wings
Gift of Finest Wheat
We Gather Together
I Am the Bread of Life
We Remember
One Bread, One Body
Taste and See
O Sacrament Most Holy

Pange Lingua
Panis Angelicus
Tantum Ergo
Now We Remain
Deep within
Ashes
Be with Me
Hosea
Be Merciful O Lord
Be With Me
Change Our Hearts

Precious Lord, Take My Hand
Jesus, Remember Me
There is a Balm in Gilead
Shepherd Me O God
Here I Am Lord
Pescador de Hombre
Go Make of All Disciples
Wherever You Go
I Have Loved You
No Greater Love

Part Three: Life in Christ

The third part of the *Catechism* is devoted to our vocation of life in the Spirit (dignity of the human person, freedom and responsibility, conscience, morality, the Beatitudes, the virtues, sin, community, social justice, the gifts and fruits of the Holy Spirit, grace) and the Ten Commandments. Some hymns that reflect the theology of Part Three of the *Catechism* include:

> "He who sings scares away his woes."
> MIGUEL DE CERVANTES SAAVEDRA

Blest Are They
We Are the Light of the World
Ubi Caritas
Where Charity and Love
    Prevail
We Shall Overcome
Whatsoever You Do
We Are Called
Voices That Challenge
Let Justice Roll Like a River
City of God

Lord You Have the Words
Deep Within
Amazing Grace
This Little Light of Mine
Praise God from Whom All
    Blessings Flow
Holy God We Praise Thy
    Name
This Day God Gives Me
Prayer of St. Francis
Let There Be Peace on Earth

If I Were a Church Hymn

It has been said that a person's favorite hymns will reveal a lot about his or her personal theology or at least personal piety. One activity I enjoy doing with groups of people who are somewhat familiar with Catholic hymns is called "If I Were a Church Hymn." The activity involves asking participants to select the hymn (or hymns) that best represents either their present spiritual state or their spiritual theme song. This activity works best when people have access to a hymnal and can peruse it for a few minutes before they share what song they selected and why. Although most do not, some people feel compelled to sing the hymn they selected, and it is not unusual for people to get teary-eyed while talking about the hymn they selected, which just goes to show how deeply music touches our hearts. Try doing this activity with a friend or a group of friends or a group you minister to or with.

Part Four: Christian Prayer

The fourth pillar of the *Catechism* is prayer. Part four focuses on the raising of our hearts and minds to God in prayer. Various types of prayer are explored and then the Lord's Prayer—the Gospel in miniature—is explored in detail. Some hymns that reflect the theology of Part Four of the *Catechism* include:

All Creatures of Our God and
    King
Praise to the Lord the
    Almighty
Morning Has Broken
Now Thank We All Our God
Joyful, Joyful
Precious Lord, Take My Hand
I Lift Up My Soul
Glory and Praise to Our God
Jesus Remember Me
I Lift Up My Soul

Lift Up Your Hearts
Our Father (chant)
Lead Me, Guide Me
You Are Near
Make Me a Channel of Your
    Peace
O Lord, Hear My Prayer
*Various Psalms (e.g. Psalm
    23 Shepherd Me, O God;
    Psalm 98 All the Ends of
    the Earth)

Anytime, Anywhere

Proving that sacred hymns can be sung anytime and anywhere, former Major League pitching star and born-again Christian Orel Hershiser admitted to singing hymns to himself between innings of games he was pitching during the World Series in 1988. In an appearance on *The Tonight Show*, the day after winning the World Series, host Johnny Carson mentioned that people had noticed Hershiser singing to himself in the dugout between innings as he sat on the bench. When Carson asked him what he was singing, Hershiser paused and sheepishly admitted it was a church hymn. When Carson asked which hymn it was, Hershiser simply began singing in a soft voice:

Praise God from whom all blessings flow,
Praise Him, all creatures here below,
Praise Him above, ye heavenly hosts,
Praise Father, Son, and Holy Ghost. Amen.

The hymns of the Catholic Church reveal the theology of the Church. These sacred hymns are an effective means of learning the faith while raising our hearts, minds, and voices to God. Sacred hymns are the Church's lyrical and musical commentaries on our faith tradition; they call us to deepen our faith, to practice that faith daily, and to live with an attitude of faith and hope. Hymns are one way—and a very effective one—to go right to the human heart, where the desire for God resides.

Practical suggestions for practicing singing:

> During Mass, join in the singing of hymns and parts of the Mass. If you have a good voice, belt it out. If you don't wish to impose your voice on others, sing just loud enough to hear yourself. If you really can't carry a tune, follow the words of the hymns and the liturgy so that you are praying them as they are sung.

> Acquire recordings of traditional and contemporary Catholic hymns (as well as Gregorian chant). Visit GIA Publications (www.giamusic.com), Oregon Catholic Press (www.ocp.org), and the Catholic Music Network (www.catholicmusicnetwork.com). Also, many contemporary and traditional hymns are available from iTunes and Amazon.com.

> Choose a hymn that you can adopt as your "theme" song—a song that captures the essence of your spirituality.

> When you pray, incorporate sacred music, either by listening to a recording or by singing (out loud or silently) some appropriate hymns.

> Recall various hymns throughout the day and hum them quietly to yourself as a form of prayer.

> Play recordings of sacred music in the background during your work-out or as you do chores or even in your workplace (if permissible).

> Print out the words of a refrain from a sacred hymn and place it on your refrigerator, bulletin board, or bathroom/bedroom mirror as a source of inspiration.

> Attend sacred concerts offered in your area by local parishes or in your diocese.

> Become familiar with some traditional Latin hymns such as *Tantum Ergo*, *O Salutaris Hostia*, or *Panis Angelicus*, just to name a few. Latin is the Church's universal liturgical language and is often used when Mass is celebrated by the Holy Father for the whole world to participate in.

Scripture

Sing praises to God, sing praises;
Sing praises to our King, sing praises.
For God is the king of all the earth;
sing praises with a psalm.
(Psalm 47:6–7)

Prayer

Dearest Lord, my heart desires for you. May I sing your praises each and every day. May I lift up my mind, heart, and voice to you in song. Fill my heart with melodies of love and help me carry these melodies with me wherever I go, extending an attitude of faith and hope to all those I encounter. Amen.

To share and learn more in a spiritual mentoring relationship about practicing keeping a song in your heart, visit www.loyolapress.com/practice-makes-catholic.

Practice 21

Make a Retreat

To be able to discover the actual will of the Lord in our lives always involves the following: a receptive listening to the Word of God and the Church, fervent and constant prayer, recourse to a wise and loving spiritual guide, and a faithful discernment of the gifts and talents given by God, as well as the diverse social and historic situations in which one lives. (Pope John Paul II, *Christifideles Laici*, 58)

Sound the Retreat!

It just so happens that I wrote this chapter about going on retreat while on retreat! I typed these very words while enjoying the peace and harmony of the Palisades Retreat Center in Seattle, Washington, in my room overlooking scenic Puget Sound! Earlier in the day, I spent some time in the chapel, strolled the beautiful nature path, walked the outdoor Stations of the Cross, and hiked down the steep stairs to the shoreline below to walk quietly along the water's edge, taking in the beauty of God's creation. It was a much-needed shot in the arm and a great change of pace from the usual hustle and bustle of everyday life.

A retreat is a wonderful thing. Unfortunately, the word *retreat* has some negative connotations. The word *retreat* has been used primarily to describe running away from a perceived danger or threat rather than facing it head-on. In this sense, retreat is a cowardly thing to do. Any military commander will tell you, however, that sometimes, retreat is the smartest thing to do! When troops find themselves under heavy fire and in a bad position strategically, retreating to a safer location where a new strategy can be devised and reinforcements called in can turn certain defeat into an opportunity for victory.

The truth is, in ordinary life we sometimes find ourselves under heavy fire with our defenses wearing thin. At times like that, a spiritual retreat is the smartest thing we can do. To go on retreat is not to run away from life's problems. It's an opportunity to regroup, refocus, and become renewed so that we can head right back into the world to face challenges with faith rather than fear, and hope rather than despair.

It is human nature to lose perspective. Often, we may not even realize how our perspective may have changed gradually over time. A retreat is an opportunity to have our perspective restored. By withdrawing from ordinary daily activities for a set period of time, we can take the time to renew our relationship with God and see with the eyes of faith. Christians take their example from Jesus himself who spent forty days (symbolic for a significant period of time) in the desert before beginning his public ministry. During that time, Jesus came to see clearly who he was, what he was called to do, and how he would go about doing it.

> **To go on retreat is not to run away from life's problems.**

In the early Church, many Christians sought to imitate Jesus by withdrawing to deserted places where they could experience solitude. As time went on, religious communities sought to withdraw from the world and grow closer to God by living in monasteries. St. Ignatius of Loyola, however, felt that it was important for all people to be able to find God not only in monasteries, but in their daily lives. When Ignatius established the Jesuits, he required his followers to experience an intensive thirty-day retreat but then sent them out into the world to serve people in their communities rather than remain in monasteries. He also encouraged lay people to participate in an adapted form of his Spiritual Exercises (known as the Nineteenth Annotation), knowing that the average layperson is not able to arrange for a thirty-day retreat without losing his or her job. To that end, many Jesuit priests began inviting people in their churches to join them for shorter periods of reflection. Thus, the modern form of the retreat was born: believers taking a pause to connect with God in the midst of busy lives.

"People travel to wonder at the height of mountains, at the huge waves of the sea, at the long courses of rivers, at the vast compass of the ocean, . . . and they pass by themselves without wondering."
St. Augustine

As time went on, other saints such as St. Francis de Sales and St. Vincent de Paul expanded and developed the practice of retreats. In the aftermath of the Second Vatican Council and its call for all people to seek holiness, retreats have flourished as a Catholic practice. Retreat centers, often run by

Hermitages

A hermitage is a place where one can experience retreat in total solitude. Hermitages are usually simple cabins surrounded by nature where an individual can retreat from the stress of everyday life and devote complete attention to the presence of God in a desert-like environment of solitude and silence without distraction. Retreatants are not disturbed except by request or, of course, in case of emergency. Hermitages are often equipped with a Bible, a cross, sacred icons, large windows for viewing the natural landscape, a bed, a rocking chair, a simple kitchen, and a porch. Some have no electricity; even hermitages that have electricity do not have TV or Internet access. Most retreatants who visit a hermitage spend at least two nights but may arrange to stay much longer. The overall purpose of a hermitage experience is for the retreatant to realize that, although in solitude, he or she is never alone.

> Three Catholic men went on a retreat together and were instructed by their retreat master to share their deepest darkest secrets, things they had never shared with anyone else. The first, after hemming and hawing, admitted that he was an alcoholic but had been too ashamed to tell anyone until now. He thanked his retreat mates for the opportunity to unburden himself. The second also hesitated, but, encouraged by the first man's confession, finally admitted to having a terrible gambling problem. He was very ashamed of his habit but was so grateful that he could finally admit to his problem. The third man told the first two that he admired them for their courage and honesty and prayed for the ability to do the same. With their encouragement, he finally got up the courage to admit that he had a problem that he'd been working on for years but simply could not conquer. His retreat mates asked him, "What is this terrible problem that you can't seem to overcome?" The third man replied, "I'm a compulsive gossiper."

religious orders, offer everyday Catholics the opportunity to take some time to reflect and grow closer to God. Today, in the United States alone, there are nearly two hundred Catholic retreat centers. To find a retreat center near you, visit http://www.catholiclinks.org/retirosunitedstates.htm

What Does a Retreat Look Like?

Retreats come in all shapes and sizes. Most retreats, however, include some degree of quiet time as well as an emphasis on simplicity and austerity with regards to food and accommodations. Retreatants are asked to refrain from listening to music, talking or texting on cell phones, surfing the Internet, or watching TV (which is made easier by the fact that rooms have no TV sets) Some retreats can be as short as an overnight experience, while others may be a weekend or an entire week. The opportunity for the full thirty-day retreat that St. Ignatius devised is available to all and is often part of the spiritual formation of men and women who belong to religious orders. Typically, retreats include prayer (both individual and communal),

Retreats come in all shapes and sizes.

Walking the Labyrinth

It's not unusual today for a retreat center to have an indoor or outdoor labyrinth. A labyrinth is a circular pattern with a cross at its center, and a person walks that pattern as a spiritual practice. The labyrinth might be a permanent outdoor structure made of stone and earth, or it could be a large patterned cloth that can be spread on the floor for walking and stored away when not in use. The purpose of walking a labyrinth is to engage one's heart, mind, and body in a contemplative experience symbolic of our spiritual journey in life. The experience of walking the labyrinth can be thought of as a pilgrimage-in-place. Walking the labyrinth is an experience of solitude and it is done thoughtfully, at one's own pace and in silence. While walking the path, one can meditate on a Scripture passage or on the stations of the cross or just use the time to engage in conversation with God. Christians need not be concerned that the labyrinth traces its roots to paganism; the circle and the journey are so intrinsic to human nature that most cultures and religions have used them. Over the centuries, Catholics have transformed more than a few pagan customs into spiritual practices (e.g. celebrating the birth of Christ on December 25). It is precisely the goal of the Gospel to affirm those elements of culture that are in line with the Gospel and to purify and transform those that are not. However, we should also be wary of any new-age thinking that occasionally seeks to associate itself with the practice of walking the labyrinth.

spiritual reading, opportunities for the sacrament of reconciliation, acts of penance, and celebration of the Eucharist.

Some retreats are silent, while others involve discussions and sharing. Some retreats are "preached," which means that a retreat director offers talks each day, facilitates prayer for the retreatants, and is available for spiritual direction throughout the retreat. Still other retreats are arranged in such a way that each retreatant meets with a spiritual director who suggests Scripture passages for prayer and reflection based on that individual's needs. These are called directed retreats. Finally, a private retreat is one that is made without a retreat master.

Some people make annual retreats, while others are lucky if they make one retreat in their entire life. Often, people seek a retreat experience when faced with a major decision or transition in life, hoping for the grace needed to discern direction. Other times, people go on retreat seeking renewal to continue in what they are doing but with renewed energy and focus. Here is just a sampling of the types of retreats that are available through Catholic parishes, retreat houses, and organizations:

- Day retreats
- Weekend retreats
- Weeklong retreats
- Thirty-day Ignatian retreats
- Women's retreats
- Men's retreats
- Teen retreats
- Sacramental retreats (First Communion, reconciliation, confirmation)
- Addiction recovery retreats
- Healing retreats
- Directed retreats
- Preached retreats
- Silent retreats
- Seasonal retreats
- Engaged-couples retreats
- Married-couples retreats
- Charismatic retreats
- Cursillo retreats
- Widows-and-widowers retreats
- Nature retreats
- Journaling retreats

Practical suggestions for practicing retreat:

> Visit http://www.catholiclinks.org/retirosunitedstates.htm to locate a retreat center in your vicinity.

> Visit a retreat center in your area to find out what kinds of retreats they offer and what might fit your schedule and meet your needs.

> Contact your parish and/or your diocesan office to find out more about retreats offered in your area.

> Get together with a group of friends and go on retreat together.

Retreat without Leaving Home

With the magic of the Internet, today it's possible to experience a retreat without leaving the comfort of your home. A variety of Catholic Web sites offer online retreat experiences that take place over the course of several days or weeks. Participants receive directions for engaging in prayers, practices, Scripture readings, and inspirational readings at their own convenience while also having the opportunity to interact with other participants by posting comments on the retreat site. Several popular sites for such retreats include www.onlineministries.creighton.edu, www.catholicsoncall.org, www.oblates.org, and www.goodgroundpress.com. Another popular experience is the 3-Minute Retreat offered by Loyola Press. This daily online prayer experience invites participants to pause and call to mind God's presence, reflect on a brief Scripture passage, and then engage in conversation with the Lord as prompted by a couple of reflection questions. In this way, participants are able to engage in a daily mini-retreat experience that helps them recognize God's presence and involvement in daily experiences. Visit www.loyolapress.com/3-minute-retreats-daily-online-prayer.htm.

> Gather a group of people in your parish and plan a retreat experience together with the help of your parish staff.

> Consider participating in an online retreat such as the ones offered by www.onlineministries.creighton.edu, www.catholicsoncall.org, www.oblates.org, and www.goodgroundpress.com.

> Make the 3-Minute Retreat a part of your daily prayer. Visit www.loyolapress.com/3-minute-retreats-daily-online-prayer.htm.

> Attend days of recollection and parish missions in your own or neighboring parish communities for a retreat-like experience of an hour to several hours.

Scripture

Jesus, full of the Holy Spirit, returned from the Jordan and was led by the Spirit in the wilderness, where for forty days he was tempted by the devil. He ate nothing at all during those days, and when they were over, he was famished. (LUKE 4:1–2)

Prayer

Heavenly Father, your Son, Jesus, often withdrew to out-of-the-way places to pray and reflect on his mission and his relationship with you. Send the same Holy Spirit that guided Jesus to guide me and lead me to retreat from the busy-ness of this world so that I can regain perspective and focus. Enable me to reenter the world, refreshed and renewed, filled with your grace, and inspired to live as your disciple. Amen.

To share and learn more in a spiritual mentoring relationship about practicing retreat, visit www.loyolapress.com/practice-makes-catholic.

LET'S PRACTICE

Author John Holt wrote that when it comes to playing the cello, one does not go through a period of *learning* to play the cello and then suddenly one day begin playing it. Rather, one simply plays the cello—poorly at first and then, progressively better. (*Chicken Soup for the Soul*, HCI, 1993) The same is true of any activity, including the practice of our Catholic faith. To practice our faith does not mean to engage in a period of rehearsal, as if warming up before the game begins. Rather, we simply begin practicing our faith, sometimes poorly and, we hope, well eventually. When we practice something regularly, it becomes a skill; it becomes second nature.

When we talk about practicing our faith, we use the word in the same way that we describe a doctor practicing medicine or a lawyer practicing law. *Practice* does not refer to a rehearsal but to the craft. Practice is who we are and what we do. To be a practicing Catholic is so much more than going to Mass on Sunday. To be a practicing Catholic is to practice our baptism every day, to put on Christ, and to recognize his presence in everyone we meet.

Jesus said, "Be perfect, therefore, as your heavenly Father is perfect" (Matthew 5:48), and a famous saying tells us that practice makes perfect. It is through the practice of our Catholic faith that each of us becomes the person God has called us to be. Indeed, practice makes Catholic!

Also available by Joe Paprocki

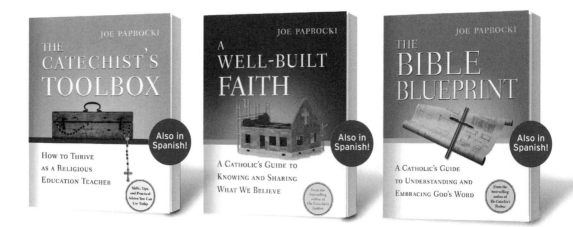

The Catechist's Toolbox

$9.95 • 2451-5 • Paperback

This book of tips, techniques, and methodologies provides invaluable on-the-job training for new catechists. *Leader's Guide available!*

A Well-Built Faith

$9.95 • 2757-8 • Paperback

From the Ten Commandments to the Trinity, this informative yet fun book helps Catholics know the facts about their faith. *Leader's Guide available!*

The Bible Blueprint

$9.95 • 2898-8 • Paperback

This nonthreatening introduction to God's Word uses a blueprint metaphor to help Catholics understand the basics of the Bible. *Leader's Guide available online!*

All books by Joe Paprocki are now available as eBooks. Visit www.loyolapress.com to purchase these other formats.